That Hood Love is all I've ever wanted

Ebony Diamonds

Contents

© 2017

Ebony Turrentine

Kola

"Kola, come on."

My father yelled for me as I cried over my mother's lifeless body. I was seven years old, and I had watched my father bash my mother's head in. I cried as he pulled me out the door.

"Why you do that to Mommy?" I cried when he pulled away from our home.

"She was pregnant and the baby wasn't mine. You might not ever understand why I did it, and I'm sorry you won't have a mother, but she fucked up, Kola, and I wasn't havin' that shit," he said as he drove off headed to the airport.

I was a kid, so I still didn't understand.

"You gotta stop crying, Kola. I'm sorry, okay?" he said with tears falling down his face.

He pulled me into the front seat and held on to me tightly. After we both stopped crying, we got out and got on the shuttle from the parking lot.

My father bought two tickets to Los Angeles, and we waited two hours for the flight, and then we were gone. As soon as we got to California, my father bought us a house, and a few of the men he always hung with moved out there too. I didn't know what they did, but my father always brought money home in bags and stuff. I wouldn't know until I was older that my father was a cold beast in the streets.

Still, as the years passed, I had a sort of resentment for what he took from me. I never had my mother to teach me to be a girl. My hair was always a mess because I didn't like getting it done at the shop, so my father gave up to teach me a lesson. When I came on my period, my father didn't know what to do. Even when I had my first crush, I wished I had a mother to hide the secret from. I was robbed of the whole mother/daughter experience.

I never even got to be mad at her for my name, Bukola Wright. Ugh, I hated it, so I let everybody call me Kola. I used to laugh because I thought I was ugly, so I figured they named me to match my looks. I never really thought much of how I came outside, and neither did a lot of boys in the neighborhood. They always had me on some sister type of shit because I wasn't all girly like most of the females I went to school with.

It didn't help that I was always alone except for some friends I had acquired from the neighborhood. My father always went out at night and came back in the morning. At 13, I was already filling out, and since I had some kind of growth spurt over the summer, I needed some new clothes.

It was Saturday morning, and my father promised to take me shopping. I was excited to get new stuff. I knocked on his door and heard him walking up. But when the door opened, it wasn't him. It was his girlfriend, Sia.

"Your father is asleep." She tried to close the door, but I pushed it back open.

"Daddy. Wake up," I yelled into the room.

"Damn, Kola," he said in a grumpy tone.

"You said we was going shopping."

"Take her, man." He got up and grabbed a stack of money out his top drawer then handed it to Sia.

She rolled her eyes at me and went to get ready.

I jumped in the shower and put on my hoodie dress and some Jordans.

Sia banged on my room door. "Come on."

I really couldn't stand her ass. She was only being nice to me so my father would think she was a good person.

We left out, and I already knew where she was heading when she got off 91 and got on 110, The Grove.

Sia lit a cigarette and rolled her window down.

"Why don't you ever have your hair done? Quinton needs to have you representing him better. I'ma get you a perm." She shook her head.

I smacked my teeth and looked out the window as we drove. I guess Sia got bored with trying to insult me and moved on to calling her friends to talk shit. She bragged right in front of me about how much my father does for her. She was just a hoe in my eyes.

After parking, Sia got out and went strutting down the walkway of the outdoor mall. "We can go in Barney's but they prolly won't have shit to fit you," she said as we walked into the store.

I was two seconds from snapping. She had hit three stores and didn't pick me up shit. I finally decided to say something.

"Give me the money my father gave you. I'm gonna tell him about all your smart ass comments too." I held my hand out.

"Bring your fat black ass on, I need to go in MAC. I ain't giving you shit, he won't give a fuck that I spent money on myself. We can take you to Walmart and grab you some t shirts. Damn, I wish your mother wasn't dead so you could go live with her and leave me and your daddy alone." She kept strutting.

I got pissed and pushed her down.

"What the fuck!" She tried to get up, but I punched her in the face.

"Don't you ever mention my mother." I kicked her in the face as I yelled.

I snatched her purse and ran all the way to the car. My father taught me how to drive because he said you never know when you have to leave. After getting in, I swerved all the way home, trying my best not to be noticed by police. When I hit the curb, I threw the car into park and went inside to tell my father what happened.

"Kola!" I heard him say before he burst out the door.

"She said a bunch of shit about me and Mama. You can beat me or whatever, but I ain't sorry," I said with my arms folded and a mean mug.

"I was gonna ask you why you driving without a seat belt on. I saw you pull up." He shook his head and went back inside.

I didn't know what to do because his reaction wasn't what I expected. We never saw Sia again, but there were plenty of others coming through to fill the space. Bitches.

My first love

I came out on my porch to sit when I saw my neighbor, Ms. Lane, sitting on her porch braiding her daughter's hair. I felt a familiar sadness when I saw a mother and daughter sharing time. It was years after Sia, and I was 16 years old and just coming into my own. I had decided to get myself cute. My confidence shot up a little, but I still had some work to do on myself. I thought maybe that's why I hadn't had so much as a first kiss. Of course, I had crushes like any other girl, but it was never reciprocated until I met Anthony.

I was in the hair store buying some yaki so I could get my hair braided because I looked like James Brown when he got locked up, and this shit wasn't cute at all. After I grabbed a few packs of number 2, I went to pay for it. All of a sudden, a a masked man came in waving a gun and trying his best to frighten the cashier. He looked me dead in the eyes. I wasn't scared, though.

"Gimme the money, bitch," he yelled at the cashier.

The Asian woman cried as she went into the register.

The dude looked back at me. "What the fuck you lookin' at?"

I rolled my eyes and smacked my teeth.

He smiled and snatched the money out the lady's hand. Before he ran out, he turned to me and said, "See you around."

My stupid ass still tried to pay for my hair, but the woman was so shaken up that she just sat on the floor and cried. I put the money on the counter and left with the hair in my arms.

As I walked home, I had a feeling that I was being followed for some reason. I turned around only saw a man sweeping his store front. The feeling didn't go away no matter how far went, but I kept going. That's until I was pulled into an alley right beside my house. I pulled out my knife, ready to slice me a motherfucker today. As I looked at the boy, I realized I had seen him a few times before. His eyes stood out more than anything.

"What's your name?" he asked.

"Kola." I mugged him.

"Like the soda?" He burst out laughing.

"No, like Kola, nigga. the fuck." I rolled my eyes.

"Damn, your attitude is all kinds of fucked up, just like your hair." He smirked.

"Well at least I ain't gotta rob stores to get my money, fool." I had figured out from his eyes and smile that he had just robbed the hair store I was in.

"So what, you gon snitch? Bald head ass." He turned his lip up.

"Baby, fuck you. I ain't the one who pulled me over here." I walked off, but he ran up behind me.

"I don't like you," he said as he walked beside me.

"Then what you want?" I asked with my lip curled.

"Ion know." He pushed his hands into his pockets. "I'm Anthony." He touched his chest, hitting his gold chain.

"Oh."

I walked to my gate and up to my porch. When I turned around, I saw him staring at me funny. He was cute. He looked like Chris Tucker when he did *Friday*.

"Bye." I shrugged.

"You go to Compton high school?" he asked and sat down on the porch.

I sat next to him. "Yeah, where you go?"

I don't know why I ain't just kick his ass off the porch. Somehow, I felt comfortable.

"Nowhere, I dropped out and got my GED."

"Oh, well I wish. My father would kill my ass." I looked at his Jordans and noticed how new they were. "How old is you?" I asked.

"Seventeen. Damn, you asking questions like the police." He chuckled.

"Well, you on my porch. I can ask you whatever," I teased. "So, next question. Why you follow me."

"I don't know. You got some pretty black skin, and I liked how your butt looked when you was walking. You pigeon toed as fuck." He laughed.

"Boooooy, your Gary Coleman lookin' ass clownin'?" I smacked my teeth.

"You know I'm cute." He smiled.

"Well, why you robbin' hair stores? You got on a gold chain and some new J's." I was really wondering.

"I needed some quick bread, and I didn't feel like goin' home. Plus, a beauty supply in the hood got bread." He laughed. "But look, I'ma come knock on your door. See you later, Kola." He smiled and walked off down the street.

I got up and went inside so I could call my home girl, Lucia, to cornrow my hair.

I couldn't stop thinking about Anthony after we met. There was something about him that I liked. He was hood as fuck, and it was sexy as shit to me.

A few days later, I was doing some homework after my father left to go do whatever the hell he did in the streets all night. There was a light tap at my front door. I thought it was the pizza my father ordered for me, so I went to the door. A smile crossed my face when I looked through the peephole and saw who it was. I fixed my new hair style and opened the door.

"I like your braids." He smiled.

"Thank you. So, what's up?" I asked like I was busy.

"I came to chill. Your peoples home?" he asked.

"I don't know you like that." I folded my arms.

"Man, move." He pushed me out the way and came in. "Damn, this mufucka nice." He said on the way into the living room.

"You ordered pizza?" The pizza guy caught me before I closed the door.

"Yeah." I took the pizza and handed him the money my father had left.

I closed the door and went into the living room. Anthony was sitting on the couch looking at TV.

"You live with your mother or father?" he asked.

When he got up and reached for the pizza box, I pulled it back and headed to my room. After Anthony walked in, I locked the door just in case my father came home.

Ignoring his question, I asked, "So, why you come back?"

"Because I told you I was."

Anthony turned the TV on then grabbed my remote and turned to Moesha. He sat on the bed and opened the pizza box.

"You got a boyfriend?" Anthony asked me while biting into a slice.

"No, you got a girl?" I retorted.

"Yeah."

"Then why the fuck you over another girl's house?" I got jealous and a little mad.

"I don't know. I liked you when I saw you. You wasn't scared of me when I was at the hair store. I liked that." He moved closer to me.

I kept looking at TV, and I felt his hand rub down my back. I was a virgin, so I was scared of what he was doing. I felt tense, and he must have sensed it because he stopped. We talked for a while and watched TV until he said he had to roll.

"I'ma knock on your door again, aight? Matter of fact, gimme your phone number."

I wrote it down on a piece of paper.

He leaned in and gave me a long kiss. It made me want more. That was my first kiss, and I was excited as hell about it. Damn, he had put me in lala land.

We talked on the phone for weeks, and as the days passed, I waited for Anthony to come back.

He came back and brought me some tacos from taco el Sinaloense. I was hooked. As we talked more and more, I started to really, really, really like this nigga. I loved how he talked about the streets and all the shit he did. It was sexy. No dude had ever paid me this much attention. He would call me pretty and even sent me to get my hair done at his cousin's shop. He still had a girlfriend, and that shit bothered me. Shit, we wasn't nothing, but of course, I wished we were.

Out of the blue, Anthony disappeared on my ass. It was agonizing to wait and see what the hell was going on with him. I started to get impatient and went looking for him myself. I asked a few of my friends if they knew him, and Asanti said her brother be hanging with him off west Compton. I got them to go with me one night. My father was in Las Vegas with one of his groupies, so I had all the freedom I wanted.

As soon as it started to turn dark, I put on some rose print leggings with a pair of ripped jean shorts. My hips were wide. Even in my teen years, my shape was bomb. I grabbed a black tank top and some black wedges then put on some makeup and smiled in the mirror at my appearance. if nothing else, I had self-esteem. I didn't care that people considered me overweight; it looked good on me.

I walked to the corner to meet Asanti and Sabrina, our other friend from school.

"Uh uh, you fakin' like shit now, Kola." Asanti high fived me.

"So, where the ride at?" I asked Asanti.

"Girl, he supposed to be pulling up now. You know how Kirk slow ass is. He can't steal a car for shit but swear he a beast."

She leaned her head to the side and gave me the yeah right face. Kirk was her brother, and he was the worst criminal ever. He gets caught for the stupidest shit. Like when he stole a fuckin' hot dog from 7-11 then took the police on a fucking chase in a stolen car where he happened to have a pound of weed in a shopping bag.

"Uh, so your brother say he saw dude?" I probably sounded pressed as hell.

"I didn't ask about ole boy, but I'm sure he prolly is," she said as she looked through her new Blackberry that her father got her. I wanted one bad as shit, but my father said I didn't need one.

"Y'all think it's more niggas our age? I need me a boyfriend too, shit." Sabrina smiled, showing her buck teeth. She sucked her thumb, and it was fucking her grill all the way up.

"Probably," I said and watched a black '96 pull up. The window rolled down, and Kirk smiled and nodded like he was clean.

"Watch we be in lock up before we pull off." Asanti laughed and so did Sabrina and I as we got in.

"I see lil bitches think they grown tryna hang with the beast and shit. It's a lil block party going on, and I don't want y'all wandering off," he said like he had authority.

"Nigga, last time I checked, my father's name was Quinton Wright. And you ain't a beast, you a pup." I plucked him in the head.

"Stop, Kola, your ass boutta be on the bus."

He drove off, and we talked shit just to fuck with him. When we got to the block, there were people everywhere. We ended up parking in the alley. I got out, already scanning the area for Anthony.

"Come on y'all, my niggas over this way."

I walked with my friends behind Kirk on Terminator scan mode.

"Bitch, calm down," Asanti said.

"Fuck you." I bumped her.

Kirk walked up to a group of dudes and dapped them all up.

"Aye, these my lil sisters. Make sure niggas ain't all in they face. Y'all niggas don't be in they face either." Kirk pointed at me and Asanti. "Y'all ain't gotta worry about nobody talkin' to this

THAT HOOD LOVE IS ALL I EVER WANTED

one." He nodded at Sabrina and laughed.

"Kiss my ass, Kirk," Sabrina said.

Taking over for the 99 and 2000..

Girl you workin' wit some ass yeah, you bad yeah. Make a nigga spend his cash yeah, his last yeah.

The music got louder, and ignoring what Kirk said, we started dancing. Shit, everybody got hype when it came on.

We went amongst other people and strayed from Kirk and his friends.

"You wanna cup, lil mama?" a dude with a scarf over his face asked.

His eyes were bloodshot red, and he looked scary as fuck.

"Nah, I'm good."

Sabrina stepped in the dude's face. "I want one."

He poured some shit into a white foam cup and handed it to her.

"You don't even drink," Asanti said as she watched Sabrina drink it down.

"Come talk to me, boo."

The dude grabbed Sabrina's hand and she walked off with him. I shook my head because even in school, she was sweet for these niggas.

After thirty more minutes, I was ready to go because I didn't see Anthony. Asanti and I lost sight of Sabrina, so we walked back over to Kirk and his friends. A smile spread across my face as we got closer. Anthony was standing amongst them now. I started to approach when a short brown skinned girl came and wrapped her arms around his waist.

I pulled Asanti's arm. "That's the boy right there. Let's just get on the bus."

"You did say he said he had a girl," she reminded me.

"Kola?" I heard Anthony call out to me.

"Why you ain't never come back?" I blurted out.

Everybody looked at me, including his lil bitch. I didn't mean to say that.

"Who the hell is this hoe?" the girl asked Anthony.

"My other girl, I guess." He chuckled and walked up to me after letting the girl go.

My bad, I got caught up doin' some shit. You came lookin' for a nigga though, huh?" He smiled, and I rolled my eyes.

"No, Kirk is my friend's brother. We wanted to go to the block party." I told the half truth.

"So, you just gon' disrespect me? I don't know who the fuck you are, but this nigga got a girl." She elbowed him.

"Hit me again, and watch me whoop your Hot Pocket head ass. I'm talking to my friend."

He walked me away from everybody else.

"She gonna snap on your ass." I shook my head.

He waved her off. "So, you ain't come lookin' for me for real? I know you did. You was waitin' for me to come kick it with you too, huh?" He pushed the end of my braids back. "Why you ain't come back," he said is a nasally voice mocking me.

"Oh shut up." I twisted my leg around, feeling nervous.

"Come on, Anthony!" the girl yelled.

He smacked his teeth and rolled his eyes.

"Don't leave, aight? I'm boutta drop this bitch off. She been getting' on my nerves anyway." He pinched my stomach and jogged off.

I watched him snatch the girl by her arm and leave.

"Look at you." Asanti smiled as I walked back to them.

"Where the fuck is Sabrina's ass?" I said, now realizing she been gone a while.

"I don't know. She still with that dude?"

We walked to the last place I saw her. We headed toward the alley, and she wasn't there. We went down a few streets, but we didn't see any trace of her ass. She probably left with that zombie ass nigga. When we got back, Kirk said he was ready to go.

"We ain't find Sabrina yet." Asanti stopped him.

"So? I told y'all not to walk off." He shrugged.

I had to think quick because Anthony was coming back.

"We can't just leave her out here. You know shit can go wrong fast," I told him.

"Damn, man. That's why y'all lil asses should have stayed around the way. Y'all said she was with a dude? What he look like?" He looked at me.

"He had a bandana over his face and his eyes where blood red. He had some shitty dreads too." I described him.

"That's Squirrel. Aight, let me see where he at."

He walked over to this tall, brown dude with a weird shaped head. They started talking, and Kirk raised his eyebrows in surprise.

Kirk walked back over to us

"Man, baby girl is gone. They say she got drunk and walked

21

off with that nigga Squirrel somewhere. Come on, lets bounce"

Dammit

The ride back home pissed me off because I wanted to wait for Anthony to come back. Kirk pulled in front of my house, and I got out without even saying goodbye. When I opened the door, I heard the cordless phone ringing. I pretended to be asleep.

"Hello." I answered with a groggy voice.

"Damn, I been calling all night," he said angrily into the phone.

"I was sleep, Pops. I only heard it this time because I had to pee and got up," I lied.

"Yeah, whatever. You good there? I still got some business out here."

"Yeah, I'm fine." I yawned.

"Aight, well make sure your ass at school on time Monday, Kola."

"I will. Love you," I said and hung up.

I hated being back home so early on a Friday. I went to the pantry and grabbed some Reese's cup minis. When I got back to my room, I turned the TV on and took my shoes off. I decided to take a shower and go the hell to bed.

I lotioned up and put on my pajama dress and fuzzy socks, then got under the covers and watched *Friday the 13th*. I had started to fall asleep when I heard a light tap on my window. I got scared since I was there alone, so I grabbed the knife I kept under my pillow.

"Kola."

I heard a loud whisper and I slowly walked to the window

with a knife in my hand.

"Open it," the voice demanded.

I saw that it was Anthony, so I unlocked it.

"Why you ain't come to the door?" I asked as he climbed through.

"I didn't know if your folks was here."

"My father is in Vegas." I noticed blood on his shirt. "What happened?" I asked.

"I got into a fight when I dropped that bitch off. She got her brothers to jump me after I dumped her ass." He shook his head and took his shirt off.

"Why you dump her?" I asked, being nosey and wanting to do flips.

"Because she slow, man, and I was gonna dump her anyway." He had a cut under his eye, so I grabbed a clean rag and wiped it off.

"I tried to wait for you, but Kirk was ready to go."

I could feel his eyes on me but I didn't want to look his way.

"It's cool. I knew where to find you."

He got in the bed next to me.

"So, I mean... you wanna talk?" I asked, being straight up.

"We are talkin'," he said like he ain't know what I meant.

"You know what I mean. I know I ain't all cute like—"

"What the fuck you talkin' 'bout? Who the fuck said you wasn't cute?" he asked with his face all turned up.

"I don't know. Everybody, I guess." I shrugged.

"Nah, don't ever fuckin' say no dumb shit like that to me again. I swear, I won't fuck wit you no more. You pretty as shit, baby. Don't forget that shit," he said with a serious look.

"Well, what you think? You wanna be like my boyfriend or whatever?" I asked with my head down.

"If you can hang wit a nigga like me. I ain't no go to work nigga, you hear me?"

He moved in and pressed his lips against mine. When he slid his tongue in my mouth, I felt my body start to heat up. He tried to put his hands between my legs, but I stopped him.

"I never did it," I admitted.

"Aaaaww, you a virgin?"

He lifted my pajama dress up and kissed my thighs. My body trembled as he made his way to my coochie. I was so scared I felt like I couldn't breathe.

"It's okay, I won't hurt you. Tell me when to stop."

For him to be a year older than me, he seemed like he knew what he was doing. He kissed inside my thighs and pulled my legs apart.

"I'm still scared. I don't want you to do me like them boys at school do girls they be doing it to." I sat up.

"I ain't shit like them lil punk ass niggas, sweetheart. I hit this pussy, I own it. You with me after. Promise you that." He kissed my neck.

I closed my eyes and let his hands roam my body. I couldn't believe I was about to lose my virginity.

Anthony undressed me and went right into kissing every part of me. He even showed attention to my titties and nipples, which drove me crazy.

"Don't we need a condom?" I asked as he slid between my legs.

"I'll pull out."

He covered my mouth with his lips and slowly worked himself inside of me. It hurt so bad that I cried, but once I got used to him, I got the pleasure. I didn't want him to stop, but he jumped off me and ran to the desk. He grabbed a tissue out the box.

"That shit hurt at first." I got up and saw blood on my sheet.

"Just get a towel and cover it. I'm goin' back in."

He smiled and pulled me in for a kiss.

"I knew when I saw your black ass I was gonna want you the long way," he said while grabbing the towel I held.

After he put it on the bed, he laid me back down. We did it over and over until we passed out together.

****

When I woke up, Anthony was getting dressed. He looked at me and smiled. I couldn't believe I lost my virginity, but I tried to play it cool, even though I was ready to burst.

"So, you know you my girl now, right?" he said.

I got up and walked to the bathroom. "Oh, am I?"

"I told you I own it," he said.

"You wanna roll with me today?" He leaned on the sink as I peed.

"Where?" I asked.

"Do it matter?" He smiled and went in my room.

I started the shower and jumped in. Anthony said he would

take me to his spot so he could get clean and grab some clothes.

"Damn, you look pretty."

He kissed me and grabbed my hand. We walked out to the corner where he unlocked the doors to a '64 Impala. Man, this motherfucker was clean.

"You stole this?" I asked as I slid in the passenger side.

He went around and got into his side then looked at me crazy.

"What kind of niggas you be fuckin' with?" He chuckled and pulled off, raising the front with hydraulics.

We ended up on Elm Street. I looked at all the dudes standing around and started feeling nervous.

"You good. You my main, I got you." He got out and came around to open my door.

I got out, and he started dapping all the niggas up. I felt a little more comfortable.

"Aye, this my main." He pulled me close to him.

They all nodded as we walked past.

We walked up to the second floor, and Anthony used his key to enter. Walking in behind him, I looked around at the small apartment and then sat on the couch.

"Who you live with?" I asked, noticing it was only one bedroom.

"Myself." He kicked his shoes off and unbuckled his jeans. "I'm boutta jump in the shower." He went to the closet and grabbed a towel.

I nodded and turned on the TV then flipped through the channels until I found *Maury*. I shook my head at these hoes who didn't know who the baby daddy was.

"Kola, come here," Anthony called out.

I went to the bathroom where he was still in the shower but with the curtain back. He set the cordless phone down on the toilet.

"I need you to serve this fiend real quick. Grab the smallest vial out the bottom drawer in the kitchen and go in the hall-way."

He closed the shower curtain, and I was stuck like I didn't know what to do.

I went to the kitchen drawer and grabbed the vial with one small yellowish rock in it. Then I went to the hallway and ran into a small, frail woman with a big t-shirt on and some socks.

"Here."

She handed me 20 dollars and licked her lips. I handed her the vial, and she scurried off. I went back inside and saw An-thony just walking into the room.

"All good?" he asked.

"So, you sling too? All trades for you, huh?" I handed him the money and sat next to him.

"Pretty much," he said as he put on some boxers.

"So, how you live by yourself? Where your mother at?" I asked as I watched him go through his drawers.

He looked at me with a distant look on his face.

"My father is in San Quintin, and my mother was the fiend you just served.

I was shocked by what he had just admitted.

"Well damn, why you don't help her? Get her in rehab."

"Because you gotta want help. I'm a young nigga, and know that shit. My grandmother and grandfather was both doped up too." He threw on a white T and some jogger sweats.

"My mother died. My father killed her," I blurted out.

He didn't even blink.

"That's fucked up," he said as he put on socks and his tennis shoes.

"I see you been through a lot. Nothing surprises you?" I walked up and kissed him.

A knock on his door broke our kiss.

"Holup."

He walked off and left me in the bedroom.

I heard some commotion after a minute, so I went out. Some of the dudes who were outside were now standing in the living room while Anthony talked.

"We boutta ride on them niggas. They took one of ours, so you know what time it is," he said and walked up to me.

"I got a bag in the closet. Go get it." He kissed my cheek, and I went to do as he asked.

I pulled a black duffle out and walked out to him. He grabbed the bag and kissed my cheek again.

When he unzipped it, there were some skeleton masks and five black .40s. I knew what they were because my father had plenty of the same guns.

"Here." He handed out the masks and even handed me one.

I started to get scared.

"Meet me outside in five minutes," he told them as they scattered out the door.

"You ready?" he asked and picked his keys up off the table.

I was shook, so I didn't say shit.

"I told you how I live, lil mama. You ridin'?" he asked, holding his hand out.

I grabbed his hand and walked out the door with him.

Cars followed us as we drove away from the building. I had my eyes closed the whole time, thinking of what the fuck I was doing.

"This yours." Anthony handed me one of the guns out the bag, and my hands trembled.

"You want me to take you home?" he asked me as he continued to look ahead at the road.

"No, I'm good." I took a deep breath. I had to show him I was down.

"Aight, you know how to shoot a gun?" he asked as we pulled up to a red light. He pulled the slide back.

"I shot with my father a few times." I pulled my slide back as well.

He leaned over and kissed me. "Ain't no turning back."

He nodded and put his mask on. I followed suit, now starting to feel a little bit excited at the thought of being a gangsta ass nigga like him. It made me feel powerful.

"You ready?" He nodded in the direction of about 30 dudes on both sides of the street.

As soon as we got close, Anthony put his gun out the window and instantly started shooting. I could hear the gunshots behind us. Anthony stopped the car, and I put my arm out and let one shot off, then another. Anthony got out and the dudes we were shooting at started to run, but Anthony's people got to them.

"Y'all niggas had us fucked up!" Anthony screamed in the middle of the street to the empty block, which were scattered with dead bodies.

As we turned to walk away, a dude ran from around a van and tried to shoot Anthony, but my instincts kicked in, and I shot him first. As soon as he dropped, I threw up.

"Come on." Anthony pushed me toward the car.

When we got in, he skirted off and hit a quick right through the alley.

"You saved my life. You definitely my bitch now," he said.

"I had to." I shrugged.

I wiped my mouth and the tears that fell from my eyes. I was shaking. He drove quickly back to his spot and pulled me out the car. Then he took the guns and threw them down into the sewer.

"You good?"

He took me into the bathroom and splashed water on my face.

"I killed somebody," I cried.

"It's okay." He pulled me to him.

"You in now, baby." He kissed me.

I had no idea what he meant by that, but over time, I found the fuck out. By then, it wasn't shit for me to drop a nigga. We robbed niggas and some more shit together. He turned me into his perfect savage.

We got serious fast, and I finally let him meet my father. That shit went smooth, and we ended up being together for 3 years. I even moved in with him after I graduated high school. That's really when I started to turn into a different person. Anthony started moving weight, and guess who was right there helping him? He gave me the nickname Gaup because he said I was all about my money.

Anthony ran the streets quick, and he took no prisoners. He was mean to everybody but me; he never showed weakness to anyone but me. I loved him so much. We loved each other.

I came home one day with a birthday card, bottle of 1738, and dinner. It was Anthony's birthday, and I couldn't wait until he got home so I could show him his real gift. I had booked us a trip to Jamaica, and I was pregnant. He worked the streets hard as hell, and he never got a break. I decided to call him.

"Hey, baby," I said when he picked up.

"Damn, it feels good to hear my baby's voice." He sounded like he was smiling.

"When my birthday boy coming home?" I asked.

"Soon. You know these fuckin' streets stay callin'. I'll be home soon. Love you, baby girl."

"I love you too, Ant." I smiled and hung up.

The hours passed, and I didn't know where the hell he was. I called his phone continuously to no avail. I finally gave up after 2:00 in the damn morning and went to sleep. When I woke up, he still wasn't home, and the knock on the door let me know he would never be home again.

Anthony had been killed leaving my favorite, taco el Sinaloense. I found out it was in retaliation for all those years ago when we made a move on those dudes. I wasn't shit but a shell of a human being after that. It took my soul. When it really hit me, it hit hard. I lost our baby the same night the police knocked on my door, so I didn't even have that piece of him. This shit wasn't fair.

"Kola, you okay in there?" My father knocked on my door again.

I was lying on my couch just as I had been since my baby died.

"No," I whispered, but I knew he couldn't hear me.

"I know its fucked up, Kola, but the streets play for keeps, baby girl. He was a good dude to you. Be happy you had him," he said through the door.

I heard his car start and then his engine roar.

I picked up Anthony's picture, and his smile broke my heart.

"My baby!" I screamed and pulled his picture to my chest as I wailed. God, I loved him. Why?

****

Months after Anthony died, niggas in our organization started trying to claim my nigga's throne, and that shit wasn't about to happen. That's why I had to pull myself together. I was gonna claim it for my own.

Right now, we were in a small warehouse having a meeting that I called. It was me and Anthony's right hand, Mitch, facing 50 niggas.

"All respect to my nigga, Ant, but we need to keep this money goin'," Jessie started talking.

"Real talk. I mean, who gonna lead this shit?" Lorenzo put his pickle juice smelling ass finger up.

"Man, I got this shit." This dude Benzo spoke up.

He was one of those big niggas who like to stunt because

he thought he was scary. He was a teddy bear in my eyes, and I would smoke his ass if he thought he was gonna strong arm me.

"You can fall back," I said, mean mugging him. "I'ma run it." I told them and observed their expressions. The unhappiness was obvious.

"Why should we follow you? 'Cause you was Ant's bitch? Hell nah," Beno barked.

I didn't say shit, I just shot him once in the head and the held my gun up, waiting for the next motherfucker to try me.

Ant, I need you, baby, I thought after I saw that I had everybody's attention.

"I know y'all niggas could shoot me down if you wanted, but believe I'ma take a few of you with me. Y'all are disrespectful, disloyal son of a bitches. I was the one who got Ant to increase your cut, and he even fronted a few of you mufuckas more times than he should because I told him to plug y'all asses to keep money flowin'. And that raw shit y'all pumpin' I found that connect, and he comin' with me if y'all wanna walk away. But right now, I don't give a fuck," I said as I looked at all of them, meaning every word I just told they ass.

A few niggas walked away, but the niggas who stayed there were my new team. I was gonna make Anthony proud of me.

****

I was walking down Skid Row, trying to visit Sabrina in the small apartment she and her cousins shared. I hated coming down there because it was sad and depressing. Sabrina kept dealing with that dude Squirrel from the party, and he got her on heroin and started making her do wild shit for money. I killed his ass on the low and helped her clean herself up. I felt bad for even letting her walk off with him that day.

I was walking past one of the open lots and saw a girl getting beat up by a dude who I was sure was her pimp.

"Help me!" she screamed, but he kept slapping her.

I felt like I should mind my business, but I couldn't. I pulled out my .9 and ran straight up on him.

"Hit her again, and watch my dumb ass work," I told him with the gun to his dome.

"Bitch, this hoe holding out. You don't know the law, I can tell." He turned around looked at me.

He stared me up and down then smiled, showing a row of nasty ass crooked teeth. I don't know what he did with his money, but it wasn't self-maintenance.

"Damn, bitch. I might put you out here. I know you can make me a lil sum."

He reached for me, so I cracked him in the mouth with the butt of the gun. He came up, and blood ran from his mouth as he yielded a blade like he was ready to fight. I had my lip curved in confusion and just shot his ass. He wasn't dead, so I let the nigga breathe. I walked off with who I now knew was Pie after conversing with her for a few minutes about what happened. I found out she was only 21, and past the bruises that son of a bitch left, she was beautiful.

"Can you look out for me?" she asked when I tried to walk off.

"I ain't no pimp," I said and turned to walk away.

"Please, I know other girls who need help too. I swear we can make you some money," she said as she held a tissue to her nose.

I really thought about it and gave her my number just in case I changed my mind.

It only took for me to watch some pimp movies to convince me it was good money. I decided they wouldn't be street walkers, though. I always thought bigger than the obvious. I called her and she had three girls ready to go, so I rented a small house and started them there. When I first started, I went home and talked to Anthony's picture and told him about it all.

I was sick, and I couldn't stop thinking that I was the reason he was dead. He was trying to make me happy, and it killed him. He got caught slipping. I started growing my dreads the day after his funeral. It was like a reminder of him and our child.

He was my first love, my first everything. He was the reason I refused to deal with a bitch ass nigga, the reason I could only deal with a hood nigga with a heart like mine. He had to bleed the streets because that how I lived.

I never wanted to love you, nigga...

Years later

"Y'all niggas need to find out how to come up with my fuckin' money. You think I won't fuck everything up in here including y'all?" I said as I turned over tables and pulled the pillows off the couch.

"Gaup, I swear we just need a little bit more time. I can't come up with two thousand dollars overnight." Marcus begged me as he held his crack head ass girlfriend close.

"See, this the shit I'm talkin' 'bout right here." I pulled out my favorite gun, which was a .357 magnum. "Y'all borrowed against your car. The motherfucker got repoed, and you have the nerve to act like I give a fuck about what you can come up with?"

I shot his bitch right in the head. He was in a prayer position and crawling to me on the floor.

"Please, Gaup. I promise I will do whatever it takes."

I nodded.

"You sure are." I tapped Cheese on the shoulder.

"Put him in that house over on Normandy. This nigga gonna suck dick and take it in the ass until every dime of my money is paid back."

Marcus broke down in tears. Pussy ass nigga.

"Come on, bitch," Cheese said and kicked Marcus in the leg.

I didn't tolerate mother fuckers not paying me my money back, and this nigga had to pay off his debt. I didn't give a fuck about shit but my money, and he was going to learn this shit the hard way. I walked out the raggedy shit he called home, got in my Skyline, and peeled out.

I rode through my streets looking at all the niggas who were out there making my money. I loved my city and the money that it gave me. Los Angeles had been my home since I was seven years old. My father was murder two years ago, but he made sure his child knew the game. It was like he knew what was coming. Even though he didn't involve me that much, with the little I got from him and the full course I got with Anthony, I was good.

I had a small fortune from flipping chickens and pimping bitches, and I had no plans to stop. I just had a house built right outside of Compton, and I loved pulling into the driveway and knowing that shit was all mine.

I sat on my couch rolling up Cali's finest bud and drinking Hennessey like a boss. I checked my phone to see if I had any-thing I needed to handle, but it was silent, just the way I liked it. As soon as I lit the tip and took a few pulls, my phone lit up. I rolled my eyes and hit the ignore button. It was Sassy, my homie from around imperial where I had just moved from. The only time she called me is when she wanted something, and I was get-ting fed up with the shit. She called back, and I just answered.

"Yeah," I said into the phone.

I heard a loud commotion in the background, and it irri-tated me that this bitch would call with so much shit going on around her.

"Gaup, you gotta get the fuck out the house. They coming for you."

I immediately got alarmed. I stood up and paced back and forth.

"What the fuck you rappin' about?" I asked.

"They over here tearing Lil Grady's spot up. He screamed your name and even told them where you lived. You ain't got shit in the house, do you?"

I hung up right away. I wasn't about to speak on such things over the phone. The house was clean, but my car was not. I had a few unregistered guns, and one of them was dirty. I ran my hand over my dreads and grabbed my keys. These motherfuckers wasn't loyal for shit. I made a mental note to eat Lil Grady's ass up when I got around the way. I opened the door and was met with guns in my face.

"Lock your hands behind you head and turn around."

I did what they said. This was some bullshit for real.

****

I tapped my finger on the desk and started to get pissed because it had been too long since they brought me in that bitch. I looked at the camera, put my middle finger up to it, and smiled. I had done this shit so many times that I wasn't even moved by the shit.

The door handle turned, and got damn, I was hooked at first sight. This white nigga with a five o'clock shadow walked in with beautiful thick blond and brown dread locs in a ponytail. He was sexy as shit for a pig. I gave him seductive eyes as he sat on the chair in front of me. He wasn't all white. I could see him better the closer he got. He was definitely mixed.

"Ms. Bukola Wright, also known as Gaup on the streets. What the hell is a beautiful girl like you doing getting into bullshit like this?" he said. He looked at me a little lustfully.

I smiled at him. I damn sure didn't look like a drug dealing pimp, but that I was. I'm sure he thrown off.

"You can call me Kola, and I'm sorry, but I have no clue what you're talking about." I put my hands behind my neck and gave him my cute girl routine.

"No, I'll call you inmate when it's time for you to be processed. Now, can you tell me about this?"

I looked at the gun he placed on the table and shrugged.

"Nice gun. I thought y'all carried .40's."

He slammed his hand down on the table. and I shook my head.

"This gun is about to be sent to ballistics with the rest of them that we retrieved from your car.

"I don't have a car, sir. I borrowed that from a friend to get home."

He smirked.

I had his ass because that car wasn't registered to me. I'm sure they already ran the plates and vin; it most likely came back to this crack head bitch name Desi. I didn't have a license, so I couldn't register the shit in my name.

"Wow. You really willing to throw your life away—"

There was a knock on the glass, and he squinted his eyes at me before he got up. He left the room for a minute and came back pissed off.

"Go, get the fuck outta here," he said with a scowl on his face.

I got up and stood in front of him.

"Damn, what a waste. You too fine to be a pig, boo." I blew a kiss at him.

He pushed me out the room, and I almost clipped up. I laughed and blew another kiss at him. I was thirsty as hell, so I stopped at the water fountain. The fine ass detective was talking to an older man. I was in ear shot, so I listened in.

"They didn't have a warrant, and since the car isn't in her name, we have nothing to charge her with."

I started laughing, and they both looked over at me.

"You think your real fucking cute, don't you?"

"Jayson, that's enough," the older guy said.

"Bye, Jayson."

I waved and went to the elevator. I got on when it finally came, and as the doors closed, a hand stopped it. It was Jayson.

"You just don't give up, do you?" I said without looking at him.

"Nah, I don't. You're gonna fuck up, Bukola, and I will be there with the cuffs."

"Don't fucking call me that."

He pushed me against the wall and got into my face. I could smell the minty cool breath he exhaled.

"Bitch, you have no idea how far I will go to get shit like you off the street."

I pushed him back. "And you don't know how far I will go not to get caught up with a piece of swine shit like you." I straightened my clothes.

Jayson looked me up and down and licked his lips. He gritted his teeth, and his anger made him even more sexy. His eyes kind of zoned me out. "You boutta know who I am."

Without another word, he walked out of the elevator when the doors opened.

I walked out and saw him get into a black '64, which made me think of Anthony's car. I don't know what it was, but this nigga's swag had a bitch weak. He looked so hood for a regular ass one time, and he talked the part. I did notice that when he got mad in the room, his whole lil demeanor changed, and his proper English went flying out the window. This nigga was faking like shit with that proper bullshit. But damn was he fine. He was at least 6'5" and he had a nice, muscular build. I could tell he didn't grow up in Mayberry; that nigga grew up in the streets, and I wanted to know more for some reason.

They took my car, so now I needed a damn ride from the station, and I was heated. I walked down to the street and sat down on a bench on the next block. It was always hot as hell, and I was sweating. I just wanted to get away from one time. Just being around them made me itch. I went to my contacts and found my uncle Tommy. He was my mother's brother and he moved to Cali shortly after we did because he was in the military and they sent him coincidentally sent him here.

Uncle Tommy didn't know who killed my mother, and to not cause what would be sure the death of either him or my father, I never said anything. Now that my father was gone, I still would never let him know.

Anyway, He lived out here when he was in the military, and he was bat shit crazy now. Well, to me, anyway. Sometimes he was normal, and sometimes he was off his shit something serious. I hit the call button and he answered as soon as the phone rang.

"Wassup, Kola, baby?" He sounded like he had a mouth full of smoke.

"Hey Unc, can you come scoop me from the south?" I said,

referring to the police station.

"Got dammit, Kola. What the fuck you do now?" He raised his voice.

I rolled my eyes. "Unc, you comin' or nah?"

He exhaled into the phone.

"Man, sit your ass down somewhere."

He hung up, and I sat on the bench and waited for him. I looked up and down the street watching for him, and this guy came up and sat next to me.

"Damn, baby girl. You fine as hell, but you already know that, don't you?"

I leaned my head to the side and gritted on this bum ass nigga who thought he could talk to me. I might have been rough, but I was bad as shit, and I knew the type of nigga I could pull. I had the body of a size 16 video bitch with a small stomach that jiggled a little, but it was still somewhat flat. My thighs were nice and thick, and my hips sat wide and sexy. People kept telling me I looked just like Naturi Naughton, but I didn't see the resemblance.

I got hit on by plenty of niggas who hollered, but I chose niggas, not the other way around. See, me, I could never deal with a 9 to 5 dude because they wouldn't fit into the lifestyle I led. I've always had this sickness for straight gutta dudes ever since Anthony, and I didn't think that shit would change anytime soon. Honestly, if I had a nigga to calm me down, I could be more feminine and shit. I had to be hard because anybody will try you, and you needed to be ready. I wanted a dude who could handle me and these streets.

"Walk away, bruh," I said without even looking in his direction any longer.

THAT HOOD LOVE IS ALL I EVER WANTED

"Fuck you then, bitch. You lucky a nigga wanna holla at your fat ass."

I didn't even wait; I elbowed him in the mouth, and he dropped back.

"Fat bitch."

He got up, and I grabbed him by the balls and squeezed as hard as I could.

"Kola!" I heard my uncle scream, and I saw people watching.

I let him go, and he fell down, holding his dick. I gently stepped over him and hummed as I walked to the car. When I got in, I saw the guy rolling around on the ground with people trying to help him. He had fucked with the wrong broad. I walked over to the car and got in.

During the whole ride, for some reason I couldn't get my mind off how hot that nigga Jayson was for my ass. I had to admit, he turned me on when he had me on the wall. I smirked and shook my head at the bullshit I was thinking. He was fine, though.

Jayson

Damn, she was sexy as hell. Her little chocolate ass had a nigga wanting to do some things to her. I knew all about Kola, but I had never come that close up on her. When I hemmed her little ass up in the elevator my dick bricked up. I've been with plenty of bitches, but her ass was by far the baddest. Big hips and shit. Fuck.

I loved a thick ass chick, but I admired her business mentality more. On some real shit, I ran this city, and she was in the way. If she fell back, all those spots would be mine, and then I would have covered the map. If she cooperated, then she could maybe be my main bitch and hold a nigga down.

I had developed a little crush on her after I watched her move around on blocks looking like a boss bitch out there. I liked her from jump, and I knew it would be a task trying to get her to like me and shit. I would make a move soon enough.

My fault, let me back up a little. I'm Jayson Wells, better known as Jay. Nobody I did business with has ever seen me or could put a face to who I was. But I was that nigga. I run one of the biggest drug operations in California. Any dope that came through the west coast came from me. Kola didn't know it, but I was her connect. Shit, I didn't know we was plugging her until a few weeks ago. That was how I knew about her and what she was into.

Aside from me being the connect, I was police—a dirty one, I guess you would say. I changed the fucking game on these motherfuckers. You have to do what you have to so you can secure the fucking bag. The only reason I became a cop was to cover my shit up. It was funny as hell working with muthafuckas who were trying to get the big dog, which was me. Watching these muthafuckas wreck their brain trying to get to me was comical.

I pissed in the coffee pot every day because I still hated these muthafuckas. But this police shit was only part time. I worked the streets most of the time. I didn't need the cops on my payroll because I was the muthafuckin' cops. Nobody knew who the fuck I was for real, not even on the streets.

I sat at my desk looking at the folder I had on Kola. At first, I was trying to take her down because Gaup sounded like a nigga. When I found out it was a female and saw her bad ass, I was blown the fuck away. But at the station, when I saw her ass up close and personal, I knew I had to have her. I was willing to make any investigation involving her go away if she was willing to fuck with a nigga. I wasn't worried about her telling me no because I didn't take no for an answer when it came to this money.

Yeah, Kola was gon' fall for a nigga, and she was gon' learn her place as a boss' wife if I chose to fuck with her on that level. I know it sounds like I'm getting ahead of myself, but I saw it in her. I like how she moved. She just needed to be calmed the fuck down, and she would be a real bad bitch.

I could tell she had it fucked up coming up just like I did. My life ain't never been sunshine and bullshit ass rainbows. More like dog shit and cat piss. I believe from birth I was doomed. I was a product of a side bitch. My mother was a black woman who fucked with a white man. A white man who didn't really give a damn about us. All he cared about was sliding into some black pussy. Unfortunately, that produced me.

See, my father was a very wealthy man thanks to his wife, Carla. She came from money, so when my father married her, he inherited her wealth.

I guess him having money meant more to him than being there for his son because he told my mom that no one could know about us. He sent money once a month just for my mom to keep her mouth shut. Come to find out, his wife found out about me then threatened to cut his financial ties. He didn't want that, so he stopped even sending money and straight disappeared.

So, see, since birth I been a problem. But it was all good 'cause I was that nigga now. I was a 6'6", light skinned mother-fucker with dreads that I kept neatly twisted. I had these bluish, green eyes that bitches went crazy over, but I wasn't in the busi-ness of wifing these hoes. Well, that was until I laid eyes on Kola. I could tell she wasn't the hoe type, which made her even more my type to wife. I don't know why, but this chick intrigued a nigga. I had to fuck with her.

*****

"Ready... Go!" I yelled as my swat team kicked the door in of a local drug dealer who been causing too much of a problem.

I don't bother getting rid of low level niggas like this, but my captain wanted him, so fuck it. Once we got into the house, nig-gas was running, but my team knocked them down. I saw a lot of girls in there who looked too young to be there as I ran through. One was laid in the corner passed out with vomit all around her mouth.

"Call a bus," I told Cherise, my next in command.

I ran upstairs where I could hear screams from one of the rooms down the hall.

"On my go," I said and nodded two times. "Go!"

He kicked the door in and we ran inside. I stopped when I saw the young girl on the bed surrounded by blood with eyes full of tears. I looked at the nigga who had just raped her and realized he was the guy I was looking for. I wanted to kill him so fucking bad, but I had to do shit 100 for right now.

"Get this motherfucker out of here."

I kicked him in the face and he hit his head on the wall.

"Jayson, you can fuck the case up doin' shit like that." Cherise ran over and cuffed him.

"Read his rights." I said as I went over to the little girl.

"How old are you?" I asked.

"Twelve. My friend was in here, but they took her somewhere." She started crying again.

I threw my LAPD jacket over her and made the call to the special assault unit. I couldn't stand to be in the room hearing her sobs, so I went down stairs and saw a table with bricks of coke. It was a nice bust, but my head was fucked up. What kind of nigga would do that to a kid? It fucks me up every time I come across this type of fucked up shit.

"You good, Wells?" Douglass came up and asked.

"Nah, work this shit for a minute."

I went and sat in the car then took a deep breath because I knew I couldn't stop myself from killing this nigga.

Cherise knocked on the window, stopping me from trying to get my head together.

"I can wrap this shit up. Go ahead." She hit the hood of the car and walked off.

I drove off and headed toward the station.

A few hours later, I found out the nigga was let out on bail. It got me so heated that I was gonna deal with the nigga myself. I went into his case file and got his last known address, and then I got his girlfriend's address.

"Wells, I know you're pissed, but they'll get him at trial," my captain said to me like I gave a fuck about a trial.

"I'm out," I told him and left out.

I got into my favorite car. My '64. I drove straight to the first address I had, and it was dead. I hoped his bitch was still at this spot.

I got out and walked straight to the back of the house once I saw the lights were on. Nobody was outside, and because of the fact that it was night, I wouldn't really be seen unless a motherfucker was being nosey. I looked through the kitchen window and didn't see anyone. After trying the door handle, I was surprised to see it was unlocked.

I held my pump to the side of me and walked in like I was supposed to be there. I could hear moans coming from the back, so I followed. As soon as I got to the door, I swung it right open. The nigga was fucking this bitch like he didn't just rape a little girl.

"What the fuck? You that police that locked me up." He jumped out the pussy and went to grab something, and I shot him in the stomach.

"Ahhhhhh help," his girl screamed.

She had to go because she saw my face, so I quickly put one through her head.

"Dirty mufucka!" He tried to charge me, but I cracked him on the head, and he fell down.

While he was on his stomach, I shoved the barrel of the gun up his ass and stomped it in. He threw up blood, and I figured his pain was as severe as that little girl's.

"Kill me, man." He coughed up more blood.

"Ain't no rush."

I kicked him in the face and pulled the trigger. I went to the cabinet and poured bleach on his body and all over the room then wiped my prints off the trigger and poured bleach on that too. I lit the room on fire and ran out the back before the smoke drew attention, and then zoomed the fuck off. This wasn't the first time I had to show a motherfucker street justice because some shit just can't wait.

The next night

I sat in the strip club surveying everything and everybody. This was one of the spots where Kola picked up her clientele for her hoe house. Baby girl was pimping hoes and flipping bricks better than these niggas out here. She was definitely about her money, and I couldn't even hate on her for it. That shit was sexy as hell, but there was only room for one head nigga, and that was me. Sorry to say, if she didn't cooperate then she had to go. I just hoped she chose right.

I sent her a text and watched her look at her phone.

Me: *What's up future?*

She rolled her eyes.

Lilbaby: *Who the fuck is this?*

Me: *Daddy*

Lilbaby: *Fuck off*

She put her phone up and looked around. I knew she was wondering who was texting her. I just laughed as I waved the waitress over.

"Let me get a few shots of Patron."

"Sure thing." She smiled as she walked away.

Her ass was fat, but I was on a mission.

"Here you go, baby," she said when she returned with my shots.

I tipped her, and she headed to another table. I stayed at the club for another hour and chatted up a few bitches before I rolled out when Kola did and followed her.

I sat outside the hoe house that Kola ran and debated on if I would go and ring the bell or leave. I had to admit, the house was nice, and she only catered to the ballers and old head sugar daddy type niggas. After sitting in my car and blowing one, I got out and headed to the door. I really didn't give a fuck about her doing this shit, but I wanted to fuck with her head a little bit. I rang the doorbell and waited for someone to answer.

"Hi, can I help you?"

Damn, this chick that answered the door was bad as fuck. She was cinnamon skinned with hazel eyes and had a sexy ass shape.

"Uh, yeah, I'm here to see Gaup," I told her as I showed my badge.

She looked me up and down before closing the door. A few minutes later, Kola came to the door.

"Now what the fuck do you want?" she asked with a scowl on her face.

She was so fucking sexy, with her thick, Hershey ass.

"I came to give you heads up. My team is on to you, and if I were you, I would cease whatever illegal business you have going on here unless you're ready to spend time eating pussy for the next 30 years," I said in my fake ass detective voice. She would soon see the real me anyway, so this shit would be short lived.

She stepped outside wearing a pair of boy shorts and a t-shirt. Shit! Her ass and them chocolate legs had a nigga weak right now.

"Damn, take a picture. Now what the fuck do you want? You know this is harassment, right?" She licked her plump, pretty ass lips.

"So, you sell pussy too? Yours, I mean." I smirked, knowing it would piss her off.

She smiled and started to walk back inside. I almost nutted when I saw her ass in them shorts. It was like she read my mind because she turned around and said something I didn't expect.

"You think you so fuckin' slick, don't you? You came here to see me, didn't you?" She stepped closer to me with a smirk.

"What if I did, though?" I slid my index finger in the brim of her shorts and pulled her to me.

She smacked my hand, and I grabbed her wrist, spun her around, and pressed her against the door, face first. She smelled like she had just taken a shower and put some of that sexy smelling ass lotion bitches wear on.

"Get the fuck off me." She fought to get loose.

I put my pelvis against her butt. "Shut the fuck up and listen. Friday..." I stopped and kissed the back of her neck. I could have sworn I heard her moan. "You need to meet me at the strip club you were at last night. 9 o'clock, and don't be late because I would hate to have to have to come find you."

I kissed the side of her neck, and this time I most certainly heard a moan. I let her go, and she turned around and slapped me.

"I should press charges against your creep ass," she said, breathing heavily.

Her nipples were hard and poking through her shirt. She was faking like shit right now. I had that pussy wet as fuck, and I knew it. She was gonna be there, I guaranteed it.

"Then do it. But you won't because your pussy already made your choice for you." I pinched one of her nipples and walked off.

I had her ass wondering now. That's exactly what I wanted. This place would definitely be on the list to be raided next. I wasn't trying to be an ass, but I liked my women submissive, and Kola needed to learn that I wasn't the one to play with. But shit, she might be a nigga's match.

*****

"Nigga, you trippin'," I told Q as he tried to explain how one of his bitches had robbed him blind.

"Nigga, how the fuck was I supposed to know the bitch was a thief? Shit, you got a nerve. What about Yolanda?" he said with a smirk.

Yolanda was my ex, and she was a sack chasing ass hoe. I swear she made me not wanna fuck with a bitch forever after her ass. This hoe was a straight gold digger. Every time I turned around she was begging me for shit. I guess she got sick of it and stole my car. She took it to the chop shop. Bitch was so stupid, she took it to my man's spot and tried to run.

I shook my head at the memory. "Man, whatever. That bitch had that scream for help pussy, my nigga."

I checked my work phone then put it back in my pocket when I saw it was good. Then, I sat back watched everybody move around out here making my money and not knowing it.

"Hey, Jayson." A bitch named Ashley walked up to me smiling for days.

"Wassup, baby girl." I looked at the curve of her hips. She was killing them jeans.

"Nothing. Just breezin' through," she said as she looked me up and down.

"Oh aight, so wassup?" I asked her.

I knew she came around there hoping to see me.

"I needed to talk to you." She licked her lips.

I nodded at Q and walked off with Ashely.

Minutes later, I was deep in her tight pussy and was ready to go off, but I held on. She had this smooth, perfect ass that bounced like a basketball when it was on the dick.

"Fuck me in the ass," she requested and spread her ass open. Her ass hole was as pretty as her pussy.

I pushed my dick in, only using the wetness off her pussy on the condom.

"God, yes!" she screamed as I pushed all this dick into her.

"Sshhhhiiit." I couldn't hold it anymore, I came into the condom.

"Damn, boo." She came up and tried to kiss me, but I pushed her back.

"After all this time, and still, nigga?" she asked.

I hated when they did this shit.

I went to the bathroom and flushed.

"What you boutta do?" she asked and opened her legs.

"I don't know. You made me wanna go holla at this bitch I'm feelin'," I said as I pulled my boxers up and then my khaki shorts.

"What make you think I wanna hear about other females, nigga?" She rolled her eyes.

"Don't go there. You a fuckin' stripper, and I know I ain't the only nigga you took home. Matter of fact, that's why I came at you. Niggas said you was sweet for it. Stop frontin'," I told her and grabbed my keys.

"Whatever, Jay. Lock the bottom lock when you leave."

She laid back, and I rolled, not giving a fuck if she ain't wanna hear truth.

I left out her spot and jumped in my car. I really wasn't feeling going back into the station, especially when I had just smoked and was high as fuck. I still had some paper work to do, but I hated being in that bitch. It was crazy seeing mother-fuckers I grew up with getting locked up for the same shit I was doing on the low.

When I was younger, I was dope boy set. I couldn't stop making money if I wanted to. At the age of 14, that brick touched my hand and blessed a young nigga. I kept that shit moving until I was 21 and even kept my record clean without so much as a questioning.

"Where the hell you been, Jayson? You need to have this paperwork on that Guap person in so we can go back at her." My captain came up as soon as I walked in.

"I think we need more. I got you, though, as soon as I think we good," I stalled.

"Okay, you been in the evidence? You smell like refer." He said as he sniffed me.

"I had to jack some lil nigga—I mean dudes up. One was smoking, and I took his weed." I showed him the roach I had just finished smoking.

"Good job, I guess." He looked at me strangely.

I had no intention of doing shit on Kola. I sat at my desk and stared at her picture. My dick shot up thinking about that ass stuffed into her jeans. *Sexy ass bitch,* I thought to myself. I tried to focus when I got a call from one of my undercovers.

"Got another one of Gaup's spots," he said like he was happier than hell.

"Take it," I said with a smile and then sent a text to her.

I was gonna push her into a corner.

Kola

I went to the bathroom and threw water on my face after reminiscing about the other night. I was over heated, and he had me horny as shit. Usually, I would have put a knife or bullet in any nigga that touched me, but he had me feeling some type of way.

I hated police, and ain't no way I'ma fuck one. He lucky I ain't no rat type bitch or I would report his ass. What the fuck did he want me to meet him for? I didn't know, and I definitely wasn't going. Fuck that. It's probably some bullshit extortion type of fuckery. I wasn't here for that shit.

How the fuck did he know where to find me? Clown must have been following me, and now I couldn't make any type of moves. My phone's text alerts went off, and I rolled my eyes once again at the text from the strange number. I tried to call it, and the person would never pick up. I started to feel like I should get a new phone now. I usually change it every couple of months. I just got this one, but I was ready to change it already.

"Li Li, go get ready. That nigga Ace coming. The rest of y'all bitches go somewhere," I said when I went to the back to grab my cigarettes.

I got curious and decided to open the text I had just received.

310-232-1111: 1 down.

I scrunched up my eyebrows. Who the fuck was this that kept texting my damn phone, and what the fuck was this supposed to mean?

I got dressed so I could head to my house, and I hoped some-body wasn't watching that shit too. I made sure Dex knew I was leaving and to watch those broads. He was my security for this house, and he did a damn good job. I was never shorted, and he had been on his shit for years.

I left and headed home. I was going the fuck to sleep so I could meet up with my friend, Shay, in the morning. We had been cool for a long time, and she would probably be the only person I could talk to about this nigga pressing me out. I was supposed to help her buy a new car because her dirty ass boy-friend sold it to a drug dealer for an 8 ball. I told her I would gladly lay the nigga down, but she just wouldn't let me. I didn't get it.

When I got in the house, I went upstairs and ran a bath. While I was in the tub, I couldn't get thoughts of this nigga out my fucking head. I knew if I didn't get this nut off that I had built up because of him, I was gonna go crazy. I slid my hands into the soapy water and started massaging my clit. I had the image of him pressing me against the door and kissing my neck in my head, and I kept rubbing.

His dick must be big because when he pressed against me, I could feel that huge ass lump on my ass. Shit, I was about to cum just thinking about his dick. I kept fucking myself for another five minutes until I came. I went straight to bed after I got out the tub and thought about what to do Friday until I fell asleep.

*****

"Shay, if you don't pick one and come the fuck on," I said, getting irritated at being at this damn dealership. I couldn't wait to talk to her about this dude Jayson.

"I'm coming, damn, bitch." She flipped me the bird.

I rolled my eyes and started scrolling through my phone. I had a text I hadn't seen from last night. It was Cheese. I immediately got pissed off and called him.

"Guap—" he answered.

"Don't Gaup me, nigga. Why the fuck didn't I get a phone call about this shit? You send me a text that my spot got raided, nigga," I calmly said into the phone so I wouldn't cause a scene in the lobby of the dealership.

He didn't say shit because he knew I was pissed the fuck off, and he was the issue right now.

"Fix whatever you have to, but move the shit and get it back running," I said and hung up.

I tried to think of who the fuck had texted me saying *one down*. It had to be that nigga Jayson. This nigga was fucking with my money now, and that shit wasn't about to fly. I shook my head as I went to the number that texted me and called it. This time, somebody answered.

"I was expecting this shit last night," the voice said.

I recognized it right away.

"What the fuck is your issue, dude? You come and sexually assault me then put your niggas on my shit?" I said, trembling with anger.

"I warned you. But I can't really talk right now. See you Friday, and wear something that's gon' make my dick hard on sight," he said and then hung up.

I threw my phone on the floor, and it smashed. Everybody stopped to look at me, but ask me if I gave a fuck. This nigga was playing games. I wished Ant or my father was still around to help me the fuck out.

Shay came over looking concerned. "You good?" she asked

as she picked up some pieces of my phone.

"Yeah. I just got a lot of shit going on. This police nigga out for me something serious, sis. He's shutting my shit down. Nigga came to the spot touching on me and shit too. I don't know what the fuck he wants." I brushed my hands through my dreads.

"Well, play him then, bitch. You acting like you don't know the fuckin' game or something. You know better than anybody how to put in work when need be. If the nigga touching on you, he's feeling you. Work that shit. Plus, you need some damn dick man."

"I ain't fuckin' no police nigga. You must be off your fuckin' head, Shay." I started to walk away.

I hadn't had sex since Anthony. I talked to niggas, but I never had sex with them.

"Yeah, but guess what? I bet all this bullshit would stop if you did." She waved over the salesman. "I'ma take this one." She pointed to the brand new Impala.

I thought about what she was saying, and I shook my head. Niggas like that don't go away. If I fucked him once, he would keep coming back, and I wasn't about to have that.

On Friday, I would be there. I wanted to know what the fuck he wanted.

Jayson

I sat in the back of the strip club watching the door and waiting for Kola's cute ass to walk through. I wasn't worried about her not showing up. She was curious, so I knew she'd be there. I looked down at my watch, and it was a little after nine. Her ass was playing games, but I was gon' show her ass who she was playing with if she didn't walk her ass through that door.

I signaled the waitress to bring me another shot of Patron. I really didn't fuck with strip clubs because hoes were nasty and had no kind of morals, but I didn't mind watching. I just didn't touch them hoes. Ten more minutes went by, and Kola walked through the door. I sent her a text.

Me: You're late

Lilbaby: Fuck you

Me: We can do all that later

She rolled her eyes and looked around the crowded club. I was having fun fucking with her ass. She headed to the bar, and I downed my drink before getting up and making my way to her.

"Let me get a shot of Patron," I heard her tell the bartender as I walked up.

Shit, she even drinks what I do. Her back was to me as I placed a hand on each side of the bar.

"Back the hell up!"

She didn't say it loud or with that attitude she had, but I think I had lil mama bothered. I had her enclosed so she couldn't

61

move. I pressed up on her and kissed her ear.

"What do you want, Detective?" she asked through gritted teeth. T

hat detective shit was pissing me off. I bent down close to her ear.

"Don't call me that shit!" My lips touched her ear, and I heard a low loan escape her mouth. That shit was sexy as hell.

"Look, either you tell me what you want or I'm leaving."

"I want you," I whispered in her ear, and she tried to turn around.

I backed up just enough to allow her to turn toward me. For someone who wasn't feeling me, she sure dressed like she was. She was rocking a short ass dress, and from the looks of it, she didn't have on any panties.

"Why do you insist on harassin' a bitch? I don't fuck with police! Shit, nigga, I don't even know you." She gritted.

"I ain't the average police, sweetheart," I whispered.

I didn't need muthafuckas knowing who I was, and she kept testing me. I was about to show her ass. I grabbed her hand and pulled her up. She didn't fuck with pigs, but she didn't protest. I took her ass outside to my car.

"Look, Jayson, you might as well be on your way and do what you need to because I'm not fucking with you like that." She pulled away, but I pulled that ass right back.

I pushed her against my truck and pulled her leg up. Standing between her legs felt so fucking right. I swear, I ain't never seen a bitch so... shit, I can't even think of words. She was nice and thick, and even had a cute little pudge around her stomach.

"What are—"

I didn't even give her ass a chance to respond. I kissed her, and my dick bricked up instantly. That shit tasted good as fuck. She let my hands roam to her round ass, and I swear I was in heaven. Just like I thought, she didn't have on no panties. Baby definitely wanted to fuck with me because she didn't stop me. I took it a step further and touched her pussy. That shit was soaking wet. I stuck two fingers inside her, and she held on to me while I finger fucked her.

"I knew you wanted a nigga. Sittin' there frontin' and shit."

She didn't say shit, but she let out a soft moan. That shit was so fucking sexy.

"Let that shit go, ma," I encouraged.

Before I knew it, she had let go, and her juices leaked all down my hand.

She pushed me away from her, and I laughed.

"Stay the fuck away from me!"

She walked away, and I let her. I knew where she lived, so it wasn't like she could really lose me. That ass loosely bouncing had me in a zone. I wished the fuck she would give a nigga a chance. I could do her real nice and show her how she could live with a nigga like me. Not even flashy and shit, but a nigga who loved her ass.

Kola had me so fucking horny I had to go fuck with one of my bitches. I called Monique, and of course, she wanted me to come through and take her out to eat so she would feel like it was a real date.

"Hey, baby," Monique gushed as she came and hugged me while I walked toward her front door.

"I told you to stop calling me baby. Next, you gonna be in some fantasy that we together and shit," I said coldly.

I had to be that way because I didn't see me with her or no shit like that, so why even let her think it's a possibility and hurt her lil feelings? And this way, she can only hurt herself because I already made myself clear. She was the only one I had like that, but they all got the same treatment. No one better than the other because like I said, they not wifey. I did take them out and shit just to be nice since they were still bad bitches, and I liked to show off with them.

All of the broads I fucked were high dollar kept bitches. Their only goal in life was to fall in love with a money bag. They didn't work, but they lived in mansions and drove exotic cars. Monique was no different; she lived in Beverly Hills and had two Bugattis in her driveway. I know I ain't the only nigga she fucking, and I bet them niggas was keeping her pockets fat, but not this nigga. I don't give them shit but dick and sometimes food. Ain't nobody give me shit in life, and I wasn't giving nobody shit either.

"I'm sorry, I keep forgetting." She looked up with sad eyes.

"So, what was you trying to do again? Dinner, right?" I asked as I walked her to the car.

I let her walk front of me because the way she looked in that tight ass shorts jumper from the front, I had to see that ass while it moved, and damn, I wasn't disappointed. She thought we were going to dinner, but all I could think about was that she had some nice, tight pussy. Fuck this.

"Aye, come here real quick." I grabbed her arm, and she looked confused as to why we were walking back to the house.

"What's wrong?" she asked, speeding up because I was walking so fast.

"Open the door. I gotta hit that shit. You look good as a mufucka."

I was already squeezing and rubbing on her ass. She got the door unlocked, and I grabbed her around the throat and bit her neck.

"Ssss, fuck. Come on, let's go in." She moaned, but now I had a better idea.

I ripped off the top of her jumper, and she screamed.

"Oh my God, what are you doing?"

"Shhhh."

I pulled it all the way off, and then ripped off the thong she wore.

"Somebody gon' see us."

I covered her mouth with my hand. After I pulled my dick out, I let her mouth go and pulled a Magnum XL out and quickly put it on. Monique was covering up her titties and looking around.

"What the fuck you so worried about? It's night. Ain't nobody gon' see us."

I turned her back around and slid into her while cradling one of her legs.

"Shiiiit!" she screamed out while I did what I said I was gonna do and busted that pussy the fuck open.

I could hear her pussy slurping my dick up, and she was all in now. She probably didn't give a fuck who heard her ass.

"Are you okay?" I heard small old lady's voice come from behind the bushes.

I started pounding her harder.

"Oh my God. Yes!" Monique hollered.

"Okay, just checking on you. I thought I heard somebody

asking for help," the voice called out again.

I started laughing and decided to just stop and go inside. As soon as the door closed, I made her grab her ankles and got deep in that shit.

"Fuck, Kola," I said, accidentally slipping up.

I was thinking about baby girl while I was fucking Monique.

"What the fuck you just call me?" she asked, trying to get my dick out of her, but I had her waist.

"Instead of Coca-Cola bottle shape, I just say Cola. That was a nick name for you," I lied.

"Ohhh, that's cute," her stupid ass said as I continued to stroke until I nutted.

We never got to go anywhere because by the time I was done, she was knocked out and I got the fuck on.

****

"Stay on her, Wells," my captain said right before he hung up.

I wished I hadn't started fucking with her on paper because now my captain thought she was a good target. Didn't matter because I was gonna lose everything we had on her once I got her to get with the shit.

I hit a jay and watched Kola leave flowers on the same grave two graves she always did. My captain wanted me to watch her, so I got paid to see her pretty ass all day. There was always shit to report, but I never did. I got curious as to who she was going to see, so after she pulled off, I walked from behind the tomb.

I walked to the one closest to the exit. I already knew it was her father since the last names matched and so did his age from the birthdate on the head stone, so I went to the second. It was a nigga named Anthony Coleman. Name sounded familiar as fuck. I saw that she left a letter, and I knew it was fucked up, but I read it.

As I scanned over it, I saw that she was deep in love with the dude. She wrote like he was right there and alive to read it. The last few lines got me.

I haven't let another put his dick in me since you died, I love you too much.

Damn, so that's why she be all evil and shit.

I closed the letter and laid it back on the tombstone.

Damn.

***

"Wassup, nigga? Why you lookin' like a lost dog and shit, cuh?" Missile asked as I walked up to him.

I always stopped by before I went back to the station.

"Nigga, you know the bitch I been on, Kola?" I asked, taking the weed from him.

"Yeah, you hit that shit?" He raised his eyebrows and blew his cigarette smoke now that I had cuffed his weed.

"Nah, I guess nobody else has either. My nosey ass read a letter she wrote the nigga. Baby ain't fucked since her dude got killed. On the way over, I pulled dude's name, and he got killed like five years ago, nigga."

"Damn, she still holding that nigga down." He raised his eyebrows again.

"That's what I'm sayin', nigga. Imagine what she'll do with a nigga like me if she still loyal to a nigga in the ground, cuh.

I gotta have her, bruh. Shit makin' my dick hard thinkin' about her."

"Baby girl is deep. Shit, nigga you need to grab that up, and you know that pussy tight as fuck. Shit, now I gotta go find me a bitch to smash." He chuckled.

"Don't say shit about her pussy again, homie or not." I pushed him and we kept talking until I went to report back in.

I left with my head full thoughts on Kola and nodded my head, thinking about what a nigga could have with her. She was gon' be my lil baby.

****

"Hey, Jay."

Tiffany opened the door to her and Duane's two-story town-house in North Hollywood. He was one of the few people who knew who I was, and the fact that he was my brother kind of held his mouth shut. He was the face I used to do business, but he still lived like his money wasn't long as fuck.

"Wassup?" I said and walked behind her as her round ass switched.

I swore she did that shit on purpose. Whenever I came around, she tried to get all cute and shit. I would never do no shit like that to my brother, but if he died, I was on it.

"Look at your fat ass." I laughed when I walked in on my brother biting big ass turkey leg.

"Nigga, you just mad because fat niggas in like Jordans, fuck you mean." He put his turkey leg down and wiped his mouth.

"Yeah, okay, nigga." I sat at the table and picked up a grape.

"So, did you ever get that bitch straight? I didn't hear shit about those corners being freed up," he said and placed his hand on his stomach."

"Nigga, first off, she ain't no bitch. And second, who the fuck you asking questions to? I run this shit, and they free when I say they are." I grabbed some more grapes. I was hungry as shit.

"Damn, big bro, I was just asking. But don't forget I'm your brother, and not one of these bitch ass niggas you can talk shit to."

He stood up like he was ready to do something. I stood up and was toe to toe with his ass. We stood there not backing down until we both burst out laughing.

"Your fat ass know you wasn't leaving that plate to fight," I joked.

"Shit, hell naw. But, for real, is shit good?" he asked.

"Yeah, nigga, but like I said, don't call her no bitch. I think I like her lil ass." I noticed Tiffany watch me talk.

"You don't even know the bitc—" I shot him a look and he rephrased. "You don't know her. You know your situation is unique. She could blow your whole spot up, bro," he said as he got back into his meal.

"Nah, she ain't the type to even revenge a nigga with no feds. She likes me too, I can tell.

"Well, don't be stupid. When you plan on getting ooff the force?" he asked.

"Soon. I can't do this shit too much longer." I tapped my hand on the table, thinking about when I first told him I was gonna be a police.

He burst out laughing until I told him how I planned to use the shit for our organization. Then it was all smiles. Shit, I was even taking big busts, stealing the evidence, and flipping it on the street. But it was time to bow the fuck out.

"That's wassup. You ready to sit me down and take back over, I see."

"You think it's a such thing as love at first sight, nigga?" I asked him.

He laughed and shook his head.

"Damn, lil mama got your mind, huh? Shit, I don't know. I saw Tiffany's ass and fell in love, so it's possible."

"You ain't shit." Tiffany got up and stepped off.

That ass, though.

"She a be aight. Did you go see Ma?" he asked.

"Nah, I talked to her. Why, wassup?"

"I can tell by how cool you are that she didn't tell you yet." He smirked.

"Nigga, why you on some mystery shit?" I asked, starting to get irritated.

"Your father called her and said he wanted to meet you."

"Man, fuck him. I should meet and kill his ass for even calling my fuckin' mother."

"You might wanna think about that shit. You don't know who that nigga might be." He shook his head.

"I don't give a fuck if he is the president, nigga. He ain't got shit to say to me, cuh. Fuck that dude," I said and got up to leave.

I couldn't believe this nigga wanna wait until I was 28 to call a nigga.

****

The next night, I was supposed to be working, but like any other night, I was doing everything but. LAPD was so fucking stupid, they let a nigga like me have a badge and barely do shit, but I still get paid. Nobody gave a fuck or asked any questions. I was thinking about leaving and just being careful with my business so I can show myself. I knew all the major slip ups and fuck ups, but damn ain't shit sweeter than knowing when shit is gonna happen ahead of time.

I was going through my phone and trying to figure out a move when I went past baby's number. I thought about how beautiful her ass looked when she nutted down my fingers. Pretty ass chocolate joints always been my weak spot. And she was a thick one too, fuck! I was about see what the fuck she was doing. I drove to the address that was on the arrest sheet, and I was impressed.

I looked around and liked what I saw. Baby girl was living real nice. The houses around there were on some rich and famous type shit. I saw that she didn't leave the hood, just moved right outside of it. It had been a few nights since I'd last seen Kola's sexy ass, and I couldn't stop thinking about her. It was just something about her, and I wanted her ass. No, fuck that, I needed her. I couldn't even think straight because she was clouding my thoughts.

I got out my truck and made my way across the street to her front door. I just hoped her ass wasn't on that playing hard shit because I was gonna feel that pussy on my dick tonight. I rang the doorbell and waited for her to answer. When she opened the door, she was wearing a silk robe that stopped mid-thigh. I could see the bottom of the tattoo she had on her leg. Got damn, this chick had me gone.

"Why the fuck you keep bothering me? Didn't you get your feel last time?" She had the meanest scowl on her face, but that shit was sexy as hell.

"Why you so damn mean?" I asked.

I was trying not to stare at her body, but she was nice and fluffy, and that shit was turning me on.

"Because you a fucking police, and I don't deal with pig ass niggas! Now leave!"

She tried to slam the door in my face, but I caught that shit and pushed her ass in the house. I know you probably thinking, *this nigga crazy,* but I ain't that bad.

"Really? You just gon' force your way in my house?" She cocked her head to the side.

I ignored her ass and closed the door. Before she knew what happened, I had her pinned up against the wall. I grabbed her leg, cuffed it, and let my hands travel up her robe. She was so soft and smelled like "fuck me."

"What are you doing?" she mumbled, but her ass didn't push me away.

That right there let me know she was enjoying this shit. Her ass wanted me just as much as I wanted her.

"Do you ever wear panties?"

She just rolled her eyes. I kissed her ass, and at first, she turned her head. But, I grabbed her by the throat; not too rough, but when she was facing me again, I kissed her long and deep. I swear I could kiss her all day. She had the softest lips. I could just imagine that shit around my dick. Fuck this, I needed to be inside of her.

As I was kissing her, I unbuckled my pants and pulled my dick out. I rubbed it all on her pussy, and that shit was dripping wet.

"What the fuck—" was all she got out before I pushed my dick in her.

Yeah, I needed to tame her ass because her mouth was ridiculous.

"Ahh shit!" she cried out. Not to brag, but I knew my skills were immaculate, and these strokes was boutta make her ass cry.

"Fuck, girl! This pussy so juicy, and tight as fuck!" I had her ass up on the wall, fucking the shit out of her.

Yeah, this shit was definitely grade A. There was no way I'd be able to stay away from her ass with this tight ass pussy. Damn, she really ain't had no dick.

"Oh my God! Jayson, stop. Shiiiit, don't stop, you feel so good." She moaned, and that turned me on even more.

I just couldn't get over how sexy her body was. I was so close to busting, but I needed her to cum all on my dick first. I hit her g-spot a few times, and before I knew it, she was leaking all on my dick. My dick was white as fuck.

I could feel my legs get weak like I was about to buss. She was gripping my dick so good, I felt like I was getting some pussy head.

"Fuck, girl, I'm about to nut!"

I pulled out and let go in my hand. I wasn't trying to get her ass pregnant just yet.

SLAP!

"Get the hell out of my house!"

I just smirked and walked into the bathroom. I knew she was feeling some type of way, but I also knew this was only the beginning for Jay and Kola.

Kola

This nigga had me fucked up; literally. I didn't fuck with him, yet he had me in my feelings. I needed to stay away from him because I saw nothing good coming from this shit. I was lying in my bed after he fucked me stupid and clenching my thighs because lawd have mercy. I couldn't believe he just came barging into my house like that, then he fucked me raw, and I don't know what the fuck he got. Now I was getting worried.

I needed to go my ass to the clinic. I hadn't had any dick, and that shit drove me crazy just now. I felt like I was still cuming.

I looked outside and saw that he was still sitting out front. I turned the lights off and ran into the bathroom to take a shower. Images of him biting his lip while he pushed in and out of me made me have knots in my stomach that kept coming. I closed my eyes, and all I saw was me clutching his strong back while I came harder than a motherfucker.

When I got out the shower, I looked outside and he was gone. The green led light indicator on my phone was blinking, so I put on my robe and picked it up. It was the number Jayson had been texting me from. I saved the number first, just so I could know what number not to answer. But who the fuck was I faking for right now?

Asshole: *Come open the door.*

I looked outside and saw that his car was gone, so he must have sent this while I was in the shower.

Me: *Can't you just leave me alone? You got what you wanted right? So just leave me the fuck alone.*

I knew I was bullshitting like I didn't at least have a little tiny bit interest in the nigga, but it would never work. He was the nigga that was trying to lock me up, take my money flow and shit. I couldn't have it.

Asshole: *You want me to come back or naw? I ain't in the business of playing games and shit. That pussy ain't been touched and I can tell. You either want me to come fuck you or you don't.*

I held my phone to my chest and debated. Nah. I didn't respond to the text and put my phone on my charger. The rest of the night, I was sitting in the backyard drinking Remy and smoking. I had a projector out back, so I put on Friday After Next and got lost in my thoughts. He didn't seem like a real fed to me. He wasn't like them other ones. I had to go clear my head. It was late as fuck, but I had to.

Whenever I felt stressed, it was one thing that always made me feel better. I drove through West Cypress and smiled looking at the house me and my father lived in. I loved driving through to reminisce. As I got closer to the school, my eyes started to mist up almost immediately thinking about Ant. I wiped my eyes after thinking about me and my baby and went home to think about this nigga who gives me chills like Ant did. It scared the shit out of me.

****

The next morning, I woke up determined not to talk to this nigga or entertain him in any way at all. I knew he was going to pop up, I just didn't know when. I got in my new car and decided it was time for me to get a driver's license. This car was in the name of one of the girls who worked for me. I needed my shit in my name from now on. I only use cars like this to do dirt in, which was what I was about to do right now.

I called Cheese, but he didn't answer the damn phone, and I

immediately got pissed. We had this new shipment coming in, and I needed him to go with me because we got shorted last time, and I was gonna prove a point. I tried again, but still no answer. I shook my head and went to his spot.

I pretty much figured out why he didn't answer when I saw the police surrounding his house and going in and out. I tried to see if he was locked up or what, but I didn't know what the fuck was going on. I went to check Note, he was another one of my loyals, but when I got to his corner, it was empty. What the fuck was going on?

After calling around forever, I only got one to answer. Lil Z. I went and met him at the playground around the corner from his father's house.

"Nigga, what the fuck is going on? Where everybody at? Cheese in some shit, and now I can't find nobody but you," I said.

"Gaup, your spots are shut down, every last one of them. They got everybody. They all gone. The corners shut down and everything; ain't nothin' movin'," he said, swiping his hands through the air to add emphasis.

That shit devastated me. My money wasn't flowing, and I knew why. I just walked away from Lil Z without saying another word. I took out my phone and called Jayson.

"So, you see now?" he asked when he picked up.

"Where are you?" I said without even responding.

"I'm busy. See you when I get some time."

He hung up, and I threw my new phone. Smashed that one too.

"Motherfucker!" I screamed.

I got in my car and tried to think of my best move, which was my next move. What the fuck could I do? I went home and paced back and forth. I sat on the couch and talked to the only person I could. I unlocked my phone, went to my email, and watched the video Anthony made me for my birthday right after we moved in.

I saw the camera move toward me as I slept. The cupcake had pink frosting with a single candle in it. On the side of the candle was a ring.

"Wake up, baby. It's your birthday, ma." *He chuckled as I stirred in the bed.*

"Happy burfday to shawty, happy birthday to my baby." *He pushed me, and I got up with a nasty attitude until I saw my cupcake.*

"Aaaaw, baby." I clasped my hands.

"I figured it was as good a time as any to ask." He got down on one knee and proposed.

I burst out crying watching the video.

He turned his camera to him and smiled.

"She said yeah."

He smiled into the camera, and I paused.

"Ant, I need you, baby. This nigga fucked me up, and I let him. You prolly disappointed in me, huh? Damn. But how the hell can I fight the police for some illegal shit? I failed you, baby. I'm sorry," I cried.

"It's okay." I heard Anthony's voice and jumped.

"Just blow it out," he said on the video.

I must have accidentally hit the play button. I took a deep breath and decided not to let this nigga stop me. I was gonna try to get my shit back up.

******

I found out that Cheese got killed in lock up about two weeks after he got bagged. I ain't been able to move shit, and I hadn't talked to Jayson since I broke my phone. I felt like an idiot. This nigga had fucked me and shut my whole life down. I had a nice pile of money, but the way my lifestyle was setup, I wasn't about to live off the shit. I needed to meet with my connect. I grabbed a new phone and hit Dirty Tony.

"Wassup man, I need to holla at you," I said. He knew what that meant.

"I was told not to fuck with you no more, and if I did, I was cut off. Sorry, Gaup." He hung up in my ear.

I got up to make a move, and this nigga wasn't about to like it. He wanted to fuck with me, I was gonna fuck with him. I put on a pair a high waist shorts that were slant cut at my thighs. It showed off my thigh tattoo that was of the roses with money buds. I grabbed a bustier and a half jacket, pinned my dreads up into a bun, threw some cute little make up on, and pow, bitch. I looked once more, and yeah, I was ready. I left out my house and jumped in the car. I didn't waste a second as I drove my ass to the station.

"Yes, Wells." I told the bitch at the front desk of the police station. "I saw police walking by me and looking all the way up my ass with no remorse.

"You can sit over there. He's coming." She snapped her neck and turned around.

"Bitch, please." I rolled my eyes and sat down on her jealous ass.

I sat in the lobby for a few minutes until Jayson emerged with a look that told me he wasn't ready. I got up and switched my thick ass hips straight up to him and smirked.

"You got time now?" I said, walking up to him and pushing my tongue into his mouth, kissing him like we were the only people there.

I stepped back for him to lead the way. His eyes hadn't removed themselves from my ass, even while people watched him.

"Uh, yeah. Come on." He grabbed my hand, but I guess he caught himself, and let it go.

A few of the officers gave me and him a look but turned after Jayson put his middle finger up at them.

We went into a room with no windows. There was only a cot and a chair.

"This your way of getting back at me?" he asked and locked the door.

"Oh, it's not get back because I have no intention of causing trouble. As long as you tell me why you doing this to me. I have nothing. I'ma be broke in less than five years. You come fuck me and then try to destroy me in the same nut. That's fucked up, and you ain't shit for it." I squinted my eyes at him.

"Yeah, well you don't listen well. Listen to this, though. Gaup is no more. You're just Bukola, Kola or whatever the fuck you wanna be called. Anything you were doing is done. I run LA, and you been stepping on my shit for a minute. Baby, I'm the plug out this bitch. You hear me?" he said in my ear.

"And you think I'm supposed to work at Dollar Tree and live in Long Beach in a one-bedroom apartment. Nigga, you smokin'," I said, getting loud and not caring that he just admitted to being a dirty ass cop. I knew he wasn't all basic and shit.

"Shut your fuckin' mouth before I shut it with my dick.

That door is locked so nobody will hear your ass gurgling." He laughed like he had told a joke.

"Oh, come on. That shit was funny, baby. I was just playin'." He rubbed my chin.

"I gotta decline," I said, shaking my head.

"It's not an option, though. You could fuck with me and not have to work a mufuckin' place. We can be on our power shit." He pulled me to him.

"Let me go before I scream," I said, trying to get him to turn me loose, but he swiped my nipple with his finger.

And I rolled my eyes as he gently placed a kiss on the side of my neck.

"Why didn't you text me back that night? I didn't hit the pussy right?" he said as he pulled me by my shorts to him.

"Let me go, please," I said, basically full of shit because I was feeling over heated by his hands touching all over my body.

"You let it go." He pushed his hand down my shorts and started finger fucking me. "I ain't stop thinking about this pussy since I hit it," he whispered in my ear.

"You gotta stop," I cried out and pushed his hands out my shorts. He parted my lips with his tongue and massaged my ass. It felt so good. He started to kiss on my chest ,and he made his way down into my shirt. He stopped and kissed me again.

"I don't—"

"Fuck with police. Yeah, I know. But I fuck with you," he whispered in my ear and pushed deeper into my pussy. "Damn, you wet as fuck." He kept sliding his fingers across my clit.

"Shiiit." I grabbed onto him and released my orgasm.

Ugh, I hated this motherfucker.

He grabbed me up and put me on the door. I could hear him undoing his belt. I opened my legs wider in anticipation of his dick again as all my bullshit went out the window. He slid me down on it, and my eyes immediately rolled in the back of my head. The only sound in the room was my pussy slurping that dick up.

"Oh my God." He gently bit down on my shoulder, making me lose my breath for a minute.

"I hate you, nigga." I came, and held onto him as he continued to beat the pussy to pieces.

I could feel his dick pulsating, then he pulled out and came in his handkerchief.

"We can finish tomorrow. Let me know what you choose by tomorrow night. I'm coming over, so cook something and get me some Backwoods," he said then walked out the door.

I couldn't fucking win this game with him. I thought he would break a sweat, but this nigga just gave no fucks at all. He just gave me bomb dick, but he still had me fucked up. I wouldn't be there anyway. Fuck him.

***

"So, explain how you ended up pregnant again? You was fuckin' the niggas raw? You know y'all supposed to strap up," I told Sherliza.

"I got a boyfriend. He said he wanna be a family, and I'm ready to stop trickin'. You know I appreciate everything you did for me," she said, wiping tears from her eyes

"I bet, especially since I just gave your ass seven thousand dollars that you ain't pay me back yet." I put my blunt out since she was pregnant and shit.

"I still got it if you want it back. I was gonna use it to find a place quick, but I think we might be okay." She pulled the same envelope I gave her the other day.

I usually didn't let these bitches borrow shit, and especially not no seven stacks, but she been on for years, and I made that shit back in hours.

I'm conceited, I got a reason, man I look too good for this necklace, and I look too good to be wearing this...

My Remy Ma ring tone sounded. I picked up the phone and saw that it was Jayson. I didn't have shit to say to his ass. He was so confusing, and I didn't wanna keep playing his stupid ass games. I was about to curse his ass out.

"What?" I screamed.

"First off, shut the fuck up and calm down. This ain't got shit to do with you wanting to fuck me right now." He chuckled.

"Ugh, I can't stand your ass." I was about to hang up.

"Your uncle got locked up trippin' in Louisiana Chicken. I saw you as a nearest relative when they brought him here."

"What the fuck, is he good?" I asked, getting up off the couch.

"Yeah, they sent him to psych."

"Man, fuck, how can I get him out?" I asked, hoping they didn't try to keep him.

"You gotta wait 48 hours. He got a mandatory hold. His paperwork said he kept screaming for somebody named Ciara."

I felt sick, *my mother.*

"Well, thanks for calling me."

"You welcome. Did you get the flowers?"

"Yeah, and I know they told you I sent them back."

I motioned to my hoes that I was leaving, left out the house, and got into my car.

"So, what happened to your ass Friday?"

"Look, this ain't the time," I said and hung up in his ear.

I was appreciative, but I had to stay away from him. He made me stupid, and I see that. I loved his dick though, and I couldn't act like he didn't have that come back. Ughhhhh, I hated thinking about him.

Jayson

It's been a week since Kola brought her ass to the station, and I hadn't been able to catch up with her. Baby girl been hiding real good, but she couldn't get away that easy. That night when I showed up to her crib, her ass was MIA. I know what I wanted, and I wanted Kola's bad ass, not to mention the pussy was fire. I had been sending flowers, jewelry, and Edible Arrangements to her. I wasn't used to catering to a female, especially one who gave me a hard time like Kola. I guess you could say a nigga was sprung, but I didn't give a fuck.

I hadn't been to work in a few days, and tonight I was kicking it with my brother and watching football when I got a text from Kola. That made a nigga perk up.

Kola: *Leave me alone! Stop sending shit to my house!*

I just laughed as I set my phone down. Now, I may seem like a stalker, but that's far from the truth. I'm just a persistent muthafucka. It would be different if she didn't want me, but she did. I decided I would still look out for her, even if she faked like she wasn't with the shit.

"Jay, I think we should consider this deal with them Muslim niggas." My brother sat down in front of me in his side bitch, Yvonne's, apartment.

"Nah, I'm straight. I don't trust them mufuckas, bruh. I already told you how them niggas get down," I told him, not wanting to keep talking about the same shit.

"We can make triple, bruh. What's the problem?" He raised his hands.

84

"See, that's why I gotta still be the brains. You know how they ran Serian shit away after he agreed to plug them. They started getting robbed and shipments stolen until it wasn't shit left but the Muslims. That's what they do. They offer stupid deals to stupid niggas, and then rape they ass right after."

"Look, my cousin runs with them, and they be on point. You need to listen to your brother," Yvonne said, snapping her neck.

I nodded and got up. I moved the table and grabbed her by the back of the neck

"Who the fuck was talking to your slimy ass, huh? You shut the fuck up when you hear niggas talking. Matter of fact, get the fuck in your room." I pushed her down the hall.

She kept looking at Duane for help as she walked, but she would be waiting forever.

"Damn, dawg, don't fuck up my shit over here." He nodded toward the room.

"Fuck that bitch. Like I said, nah, we ain't doin' the shit. I'm boutta step outside and holla at Missile and them."

I dapped him up and headed out. We grew up on Crenshaw, and that's where we hung sometimes, but we went to Watts on Grape a lot too in the Jordan downs. We used to go see my aunt when she lived there, and it just stuck with us. People heard I was police and stopped fuckin' with me except the people who really knew me better.

When I got outside, niggas were everywhere as usual. I saw some of my homies huddled around laughing and shit.

"Jay, what's good, cuh?" Missile ugly ass walked up and dapped me. He had half his teeth missing, and his hair was in this wild ass crazy bush that he refused to do shit with at all.

"Don't shoot." His lil cousin Rico came up to me too.

"Shut the fuck up, nigga. It's niggas like me who put that word out for y'all niggas so you won't get knocked. Y'all gon' miss this badge." I took the weed out of Missile's hand and pulled.

"So, you ready to come back to the hood or something, nigga?" Missile asked.

"Somethin' like that." I handed him his shit back.

"That's wassup."

"Damn, y'all niggas workin' with the feds now?"

A nigga I didn't recognize walked up trying to look intimidating, but he was a sweet nigga.

"You might wanna watch your motherfuckin' mouth, homeboy," I said, ready to pull my shit out my waist.

"Mex, you need to fall back, bruh. This the big homie, Jay." Missile motioned toward me.

He looked at me because he knew the situation was gonna be fucked up in a minute. Me and Missile grew up from lil corner boys together, and he knew the kind of hell I brought.

"I don't give a fuck what he used to be. Bacon is bacon, my nigga. That shit ain't a good look," he said looking at me with a mean mug. I smiled though.

"I'm boutta take a walk, lil nigga," I told Missile.

He knew what I meant. I went to the alley down 104th and waited until I heard the whistle. I couldn't do shit in public right now, but I damn sure could handle it on the low.

A few minutes passed and I heard footsteps then the sound I was waiting for. Missile whistled, letting me know we were good. I came out the cut smoking a Black and Mild and holding my pretty bitch, a Desert Eagle. It was my favorite.

"What's wrong, nigga? You ain't want motherfuckers to see how you get down?" the nigga asked, looking scared on the low.

"Nah, I'm one time, remember?"

I put a bullet right between his eyes.

Missile went one way, and I went another.

I don't tolerate disrespect of any kind from a fucking soul, and I wasn't about to start now. As soon as I got in my car, I heard them call for police to the scene that I had just made. I chuckled and drove my ass off. He should have shut his fuckin' mouth.

*****

I had been watching the way Kola did shit, and while she was smart with most of the shit she did, she was also dumb with some. She didn't know that I was watching her along with a few other muthafuckas. The good thing was that I was on her side, and this nigga who was trying to come up off her was about to meet his maker. This girl played so damn hard, but in reality, she wasn't built for this hardcore shit. I planned to change that.

I wouldn't make her completely leave the game, but I was gon' make sure her ass was prepared for pussy niggas like this one who I was about to kill.

"So, you thought you was about to get paid, huh? My bad, did I fuck up yo gig?"

He looked scared as hell, and that shit was funny as fuck to me. I cocked my gun back and this bitch ass nigga pissed on his self.

"You should have been more careful, playboy." I sent two through his dome and walked away like I had never been there. I texted her and told her she needed to watch her back.

Lilbaby: You so annoying

Me: It was a nigga following you.

Lil baby: Yeah, your ass. we need to talk anyway.

I got excited as hell. I knew she would change her mind.

Me: when?

Lil baby: I'll find you.

I smiled, feeling confident as hell. I knew her sexy ass would come around.

*****

"Damn, Jay, shit."

Monique was throwing that ass back, and the sound of her ass clapping against me had me ready to cum quicker than I planned. I slowed down before I fucked up. She had that tight pussy, and it was pulling my dick like a vortex.

"Do a split on it." I lay back and she slid down into a split then started bouncing her ass like a stripper hoe.

I loved to see the curve of her ass as it went up and down.

"I wanna have your baby, daddy." She moaned, causing my dick to go soft.

I pushed her off me and got up.

"What's wrong?" she asked like she didn't know.

"Don't say no shit like that to me. I don't want no kids with you, what the fuck?"

I wished like hell I didn't bring her to my place because I couldn't just leave.

"Why, Jay? We been doing this shit, and I think it's time—"

"Nope, bye man. I asked you so many times not to think of us as shit but dick and pussy, but you can't, so we gotta cut shit off. No, I ain't boutta sit here while you cry and get dramatic either, so you can go head."

"Fuck you, then, nigga. I got ballers on speed dial." She scooted off the bed and got up to get dressed.

"Good, because I wouldn't buy you a pack of paper plates from Dollar Tree, bitch. Get your scum ass out my house." I turned to the dresser and saw her ass in the mirror as she walked away.

My dick jumped back up.

"I didn't ask you for shit, which means I really liked you, nigga. I guess you was right, though, I caught feelings for a ain't shit nigga." She wiped her face.

"My bad, aight? I ain't mean to hurt your feelings, but I begged you not to get your heart mixed up with fuckin'. Now I lost some good ass pussy," I said to her.

I could tell she ain't hear shit but the fact that I said she had good pussy, and she started smiling. I couldn't get through to her ass.

I was about to go shower when I heard knocking on the door, which pissed me the fuck off because nobody should be at my door. I went to the peephole, and a smile crept across my face, then it disappeared when I realized Monique's ass was upstairs.

I opened the door ass naked and watched as Kola's eyes dropped down to my dick.

"I would have shot through the door if you was anybody else, baby. Damn, I ain't think I was gonna be able to catch up to you." I smiled as my neighbor passed and ran off after seeing me.

I backed up and let Kola walk in.

"You can put some clothes on."

She rolled her eyes and acted like she wasn't loving the view. I smiled and ran upstairs quickly to throw on some shorts and a shirt. Monique was about to walk past when I stopped her.

"Eat shit, Jay." She yanked away from me before I said anything.

I burst out laughing and smacked her on the ass. "You know when you get home you gonna be thinkin' about a nigga." I put on some shorts but opted out of putting on a shirt.

She gritted on me and walked down the stairs, and I was right behind her.

Kola watched in envy as Monique walked past. She smirked and sat back on the couch.

"I could have come back if you were busy." Kola crossed her legs.

"Wow, you truly ain't shit." Monique walked out the door.

"You really ain't," Kola agreed with her.

"So, why you here, and how the fuck you know where I stay?" I asked and sat on the couch next to her.

She fake scooted over.

"You think you the only one with connections? I need help. Since your punk ass got me in a spot, I need your help."

"Don't make me pop your ass in the mouth for being disrespectful, real talk."

She smacked her teeth and looked at me, unbothered by my threat.

"Anyway, I need a cut of your profits for stepping on my business like you did," she said boldly.

"You must have lost your fuckin' mind. You disappear and come talkin' 'bout taking money from me? You wired or something?" I asked, feeling suspicious.

I ripped her shirt off and didn't see shit but those big ass chocolate titties.

"Fuck, I can give you half of everything if you marry a nigga," I said and squeezes one of her titties.

She popped my hand.

"Why the hell you tear my shirt? I ain't got shit to wear now. And no, I want 25% for the next year." She took off what was left of her shirt off.

"Hell no. You know how much money that would be?" I couldn't help but attack her neck, planting kisses that made her moan.

"I ain't fuckin' you."

Kola pushed me off, but when she did, one of her nipples slipped out her bra.

"I bet you don't have no draws on, do you." I quickly took her nipple into my mouth, and she grabbed the back of my head and spread her legs.

I looked under the skirt and saw that she had on a thong.

I didn't finish with Monique, but I could get Kola in the shower and clean up before I fuck. I started kissing her thighs and found myself face to face with her pussy. I couldn't believe she was letting me do this shit. After yanking her down, I moved her thong aside and tasted her sweet pussy. Oh my God. It was like sweet cream.

"Sssss." She arched her back, and I grabbed one of her titties and squeezed. I wanted her to cum, so I started probing in and out of her pussy hole with my tongue, then gently sucked on her clit.

"Yes, keep goin'. Oh my God." She jumped on my face and came so hard she almost broke my neck.

"Got damn," she said breathlessly.

"Let me get in the shower so I can feel that pussy." I got up and wiped my face.

"Um, I told you I wasn't fuckin' you. I wasn't playin'." She got up and fixed her clothes.

"You got me fucked up. You think you gonna get the head and bounce?" I asked, getting pissed.

"You probably just fucked that bitch who just left, and you think I'm boutta fuck you. Uh no, now you know what it's like to get fucked. 25%, and we might can go on a date." She squeezed my hard dick and smirked before walking out.

"This bitch just played me," I said to myself then chuckled.

Kola was tripping like shit, though. Why the fuck would I pay her? I jumped in the shower and got dressed. Of course, Kola was on my mind. She came in here demanding shit. I didn't know what the fuck it was about her ass, but I couldn't let the shit go. I hadn't seen her because she had been dodging, and I still got down and licked that pussy. I kicked myself for that clown shit and went ahead to finish my day.

Kola

I decided to play my own game with Jay. I knew for a fact that he was thinking about giving me whatever I wanted so he could get some of this pussy. He was gonna play tough for a minute, but he would fold. I felt so good, I was going to get my toes and shit done so I could be cute for this little cabaret party I was going to with Shay and our friend Diamond.

It really wasn't my scene, but I didn't have shit else to do tonight.

I went to Ms Song nails and waited impatiently for somebody to take me. I looked out the window and jumped up when I saw this nigga I used to talk to, Derrick, talking on his phone and smiling his trifling ass off. I should have killed him after how he tried to play me, but I said fuck it, he wasn't worth the charge. I tried to hide my face, but I caught his eye and he walked in like he was furious.

"Kola, what the fuck?" He then he put on that million dollar trap he called a smile. It makes your heart melt, but fuck him.

"I told you to kill yourself a long time ago. Still holding on, I see." I rolled my eyes and tried not to look at the dick print that stood between us.

"You never even told me what I did wrong, girl. I called you, and you just basically cut me off without notice." He shrugged and scrunched his face up into this cute ass frown.

God, I hated his sexy ass.

"Without warning? Derrick, you had a bitch pregnant and

thought I wouldn't find out. I saw y'all at the mall, and instead of killin' you right there in public, I cut you off."

"What? I only got one kid, and you knew about that. I ain't have no bitch pregnant back then." He turned his face up looking confused.

"Y'all niggas will lie like you ain't been caught. I saw you going into Edible Arrangements with the bitch, and she was damn sure pregnant," I reminded him.

"Oh shit." He burst out laughing and clapping his hands.

"I wish the fuck you would have just walked up on us, then you would have met my sister." He went through his phone and showed me a Facebook picture of him, the girl, and a couple of old people.

"That don't prove shit." I shook my head.

"Okay, how 'bout this one." He put the phone back to my face, and it was a set of twins, boy and girl, with a caption.

We came into this world together, happy birthday twin. #twins #fraternal

I pushed the tagged person, and it was indeed the girl. She was his twin sister.

"You never told me you had a sister, and nigga, I wasn't even on your Facebook." I smacked my teeth, now feeling like a jack ass.

"That's because you never wanted to meet my family, remember?" He sat down and scooted closer, showing those dimples as he grinned.

I traced his face to search for any dishonesty, and there was none.

"I see you grew a beard," I said, looking ahead and not at him.

"So, you just gonna act like you don't owe a nigga an apology?" He nudged my leg.

"I don't. Y'all niggas play all day. It would have just been a matter of time." I looked at him.

"That's fucked up. Whatever then. See you around."

He got up, and I watched his 6'2" 290 pound ass walk toward the door. He stopped and came back.

"Can I call you? I need your new number," he demanded.

I pushed air through my nose then grabbed his phone and keyed my number in.

"I'ma hit you, aight? You need to make it up." He came down and whispered in my ear. "You owe me some now."

I rolled my eyes because if nothing else, that nigga had a Mandingo. Even though I never let him use it, I did see it when he sent pics and shit. I was so stuck on not letting a nigga touch me back then because I didn't wanna disrespect what Anthony called his. I know it sounds stupid, but shit, my feelings are my feelings, and I didn't give a fuck what nobody thought.

"You said a phone call." I smirked.

"We ready for you." The Asian lady came up.

"Here, it's on me." Derrick took out a wad of cash, peeled off five one hundred dollar bills, and handed them to me.

"I see business is still good." I walked past him and hit his dick with my ass on purpose.

"Damn," I heard him say as I sat down. "I'ma call you, aight?" He smiled and backed out the door.

I wished now that I would have said something that day. We used to be lit together. He was a gun supplier, and with the fact that he was God sexy, I didn't stand a chance when I started buying from him. I chose to fuck with him, and it was worth it until that day I saw him in the mall. I guess talkin' on the phone wouldn't hurt shit.

****

I stared myself down in the mirror and enjoyed the view. I had on a black and yellow catsuit with a pair of black and yellow Jordans I had special ordered when I bought the outfit. I wasn't a heel type of girl, so most of the time I rocked tennis shoes. I turned and saw how my ass popped out, and knew I was fire.

I heard my doorbell ring, and I knew it was Diamond. She said she was gonna leave her house soon, and she didn't live that far. I looked through the peephole and opened the door for her.

"Wooooh, honey, them bitches gonna side eye that ass all night," Diamond snapped and sat on the chair.

"Girl, you lookin' bomb as usual." I admired her blue and white Bermuda shorts.

My phone vibrated, and I smirked at the text.

Asshole: 15?

This nigga Jayson was still trying his ass off, but I couldn't help but enjoy the effort. I didn't sell pussy, so if he agreed, I still didn't have to fuck him if I didn't want to.

"Who got you smiling over there?" she asked and pulled the bottle of Remy out the bag she brought in.

"Girl, this nigga," I said, not wanting to give up too much information.

I didn't respond to the text. Instead, I sat and talked shit with Diamond until Shay came to join us. We had some drinks and thought about smoking, but decided to wait until we were outside the spot.

"So, what happened with you and that police dude?" she asked.

"Nothing," I said as I sprayed perfume on and looked in the mirror one more time before pulling off.

"You need a man, Kola. Jesus, we were starting to think you liked pussy." Her and Diamond laughed.

"Well, since you wanna know, me and Derrick started talking a little bit."

I didn't care if they knew about Derrick, but I didn't want to talk to them about Jayson. Being who I was, and regardless of what Shay said, me fucking and being with a nigga from LAPD wouldn't look right on my part.

"But, I thought—" Diamond started.

"No, I was wrong as hell. I don't know, though, I don't feel the way I did before. Maybe it's been too long," I said and finally pulled off.

"So, back to the police dude," Shay said, pressing the issue.

"Ughh, damn. We fucked, it was bomb, and he wanna fuck with me, but I want to replace my losses," I snapped.

"Bullshit. You don't wanna talk about him for a reason. He got in your head."

Shay was getting on my damn nerves. I didn't even respond to her ass. I kept driving, and we pulled into the first spot I saw outside of the warehouse. I pulled out the shit I rolled first, and we smoked it down then lit the others. We were good and lit when we got out.

"I already see some fine niggas stomping in there." Diamond

perked her titties up and started her stank walk, as I called it. She poked her ass out and crooked one hand, letting her ass bounce from how hard she switched her hips.

"Bitch, please stop embarrassing us," I told her and slapped her hand down.

"Shhhhhh." Shay hushed us as this big linebacker type nigga walked by us.

"Your ass thirsty as fuck, man," I told her.

"Girl, you enjoy those fingers in your pussy forever. I will take me a big Jethro hood nigga any day." She side eyed me.

"Whatever."

I got onto the delivery elevator with everybody else and looked through my phone at both texts I had just received; one was from Derrick and one from Jayson.

Derrick: *So when you gonna let me come see your black ass.*

I smiled and then opened Jayson's new text.

Asshole: *15 ½*

Oddly and idiotically enough, I decided to text Jayson back.

Me: *I see you not getting it, bye Jayson.*

When he didn't respond, I felt like our little game was over. I started to panic, thinking he was over it. But I wanted him to leave me alone, didn't I?

I didn't really feel like dancing much once Jayson didn't hit me back after our exchange. I kept looking to see if he texted back, and nothing.

"You good, Kola?" Shay yelled into my ear over the music.

"Yeah, I need some more drinks." I went straight to the bar and ordered some Bacardi Margaritas.

I took down mine as soon as the bartender set the bitch down.

"Gimme another one," I said as my friends watched in horror.

I kept taking down drinks and got too drunk. I went to the bathroom and pulled out my phone. The only thing I could remember after that was Diamond coming into the stall.

"Shit, Kola, you can't even stand up," Diamond said as my phone started ringing.

I couldn't even answer it I was so drunk.

"Hello." Shay snatched my phone and answered. "She fucked up drunk, we about to take her home," she told whoever it was.

I opened my mouth to ask who called, but I threw up all over Diamond's shoes.

"Oh my God, Kola!" she yelled before I hit the floor and passed out.

****

My eyelids fluttered as I tried to adjust my sight to my surroundings. I knew I wasn't home, so where the fuck was I? I tried to sit up, and my head started spinning, causing me to lay back down on the green and black decorated pillow. It was a nice ass bedroom; the decor most definitely wasn't from the cheap spots.

I turned to my right and screamed when I saw Jayson snoring in my face. I fought through this ass kicking hangover and went to find my damn clothes. Of course, I couldn't find the shit for nothing. I was ass hole naked and pissed that he probably fucked me, and I didn't know it.

"That's my breakfast in bed?" he asked as he watched at me walk across the room.

"How the hell did I get here, and why am I naked?" I yelled at him.

"Your ass threw up all over your clothes. I washed you up and gave you that sweat suit right there. You passed back out, and now here we are." He yawned.

"Well, I'm ready to go home. Where my friends?" I picked up the sweat suit and saw that it had vomit all over it.

"You threw up on that too. What the fuck was you drinkin', girl?" Jayson asked as he got up and stretching. He had on sweat pants and a shirt.

"Liquor, duh." I waved him off and got back in the bed since I didn't have any damn clothes.

"Your mouth, man." He shook his head. "Who is Derrick?" he asked me.

I turned my head to the side, wondering why the fuck he was asking me anything.

"My nigga, why?" I lay down and smirked at my response.

"Nah, he ain't. You would have been screamed you had a man."

He had my ass there.

"Well, he's my ex, but we boutta be back on," I told him.

"Bullshit, so why you playin' stupid ass games with me then. I know you was sick when I ignored your ass. I only called because you called me first." He came out the bathroom and jumped back in the bed with me.

"I didn't call you."

"Yeah, you did." He pulled out his phone and hit a button.

"Why you gotta be a police, boo? I like yooooouuuu, I need you, Jayson."

I heard myself whining in the phone. What the fuck? I didn't even remember that shit.

"That was an accident," I said and held my stomach because I started to feel sick.

He left the room and came back in carrying a Tylenol bottle and a ginger ale.

I cut my eyes at him before taking the soda and pills from his hand.

"Thank you," I told him and took two of the Tylenol.

"Damn, I got a thank you, huh?" He yawned.

"So, I need to wear some of your shorts and a shirt. I'm ready to go my ass home," I said

"It's 4:48 in the damn morning. I'm takin' my ass back to bed, and I'll think about it when I wake up." He threw his arm around me and slowly started to fade back to sleep.

"Jay, wake your ass up." I nudged him, but I didn't have the power to fight him.

I slid back down and went my ass back to sleep too, but when I woke up, I was gone for sure, I convinced myself.

My second time waking up was a lot better than the first. Jay was now gone, and there was a bag from Balmain. I opened it and smiled at the gesture. His ticket was high as fuck for this shit too. He left the receipt in the bag with a note.

I hope you like it

Jay

I pulled out the dress, and his taste wasn't bad for a dude. It was long, flowing, and an awkward shade of purple. It was beautiful. I got off the large bed and stepped on a shoe from Manolo and quickly opened the box.

"Oh my God." I picked up the diamond lit shoes.

No man had ever bought me shit. Niggas thought that since I had some weight on me, they could treat me any kind of way. Fuck that, I started demanding my respect, and yeah, I went on dates and shit, but none of them ever gave me shit like this. Anthony, of course, showered me with any and everything I wanted. I started to feel sick thinking about him. I hated when I did this to myself. Everything is compared to him. I straightened up and admired the gifts.

I slightly smiled because while I wanted to be all hard and shit, he made me smile, and it felt so wrong because he was the wrong dude to do it. Right?

I picked up my phone to thank him, and I already had a text.

Asshole: I wish I didn't have to roll out. If you want to leave, take the Lambo. Keys in the drawer.

Of course I wanted to leave, I told myself, so I texted him back.

Me: I don't even know what to say. Thank you.

Smiling, I locked my phone and decided to grab one of his shirts and put it on while I walked around his house. He lived modest as hell; I guess he couldn't be too flashy, though, because people start asking questions and his ass would be under investigation.

I went to the kitchen and saw that he didn't have any damn food at all in his fridge. I shook my head because I damn sure could use something to eat.

"Damn men."

I shook my head and went back into the room and turned the TV on. I went through his drawers and found me some damn weed and some rollups. I clapped my hands because I sure could use something to tighten my ass up right now. I rolled up and laid back watching TV in this nigga's bed like I lived here. My dumb ass didn't think about the munchies, and the fact that he ain't have no food in his damn house irritated my life.

I went to the shower and got clean then put on the dress and shoes. I felt over done as fuck, but I didn't have shit else to wear. The keys were right where he said, but I looked around for a spare key to the house so I could get back in. He had one in the kitchen drawer.

When I got to his driveway, I unlocked the doors to the Lambo and slid in. This bitch was nice as hell too. I went in the glove box and saw that the registration wasn't in his name. Smart nigga there. This car would certainly put him on the radar.

After starting it up, I pulled off, and instead of going home, I went to the grocery store. My phone rang and I saw that it was Shay calling.

"Hey, boo," I said, holding the phone between my ear and shoulder.

"Biiiiiiitch, if that's the Jayson you not sure about talking to, you a dumb bitch. Chile, he scooped your ass up and pulled off like you was his baby. I like him," she screamed into the phone.

"Okay, calm down. Just cuz he cute don't mean shit," I said like I wasn't about to grocery shop for this nigga.

"Oh boo, it's okay to be in denial. But for real, I say, fuck Derrick. That nigga Jayson's presence spoke volumes to his gangsta swag. I swear, it was just like you said. He ain't no regular ass police." She sounded like she had a damn crush.

"Well, you fuck with him then," I snapped like I had an attitude.

"Oooop, well I guess he taken." She laughed.

"Oh my God, you irritatin'." I exhaled and turned into the shopping center.

"So, where you at? I wanna come through so I can laugh you out for that drunk shit in person," she continued.

"I'm not home yet. I had to stop at the store." I told a half truth.

"Did you fuck him?" she asked sounding excited.

"Shay!" I yelled at her.

"Okay, damn, just call me when you get home," she said in a sad tone.

"I'm sorry. I like him, Shay, I just—"

"Fuck him being what he is, you already know that shit a front, sis. That nigga built for more than that, and you know it. Just give the nigga a chance, boo. What the fuck is there left to lose? I'm boutta just go hang with my cousin, aight. Hit me later." She hung up.

I got out the car with my mind going all over the place. I felt the vibrations from my phone and I looked to see Derrick calling me. Lord, I was popular today.

"Hey, Derrick." I put on a semi upbeat tone.

"What's good? I was hoping to catch up to you today." His baritone voice was so sexy and smooth.

"Aaaaw, well, I can call you tonight." I smiled.

"Who the fuck is that!" I heard a female say in the background.

"Shit." Derrick hung up, and I squinted at the phone like he could see me.

He called back, and I answered in my savage bitch tone.

"Nigga," I answered, ready to snap on his ass in front of this damn store.

"Who the fuck is this?" a female yelled into the phone.

"Bitch you called me. Your mother ain't teach you manners?' I turned my lip up.

"Hoe, this his girlfriend," she said before I heard scuffling.

"Bitch, gimme my fuckin' phone," I heard Derrick yell. "How the fuck you get in my apartment?" I heard him say.

"You can't quit me, motherfucker."

I heard blows landing, and I just hung up. I wasn't with nobody's drama, and clearly this nigga had a bitch or just got rid of one. He wasn't available for nothing but fucking in my book now. He called back, and I didn't know if it was him or the girl, so I let it go to voicemail. He kept calling back as I went through the fruits and vegetables, so I just picked up.

"What mufucka!" I yelled.

"Damn, what I do now? I was just seeing if you was feeling better. I see I gotta still work on that mouth," Jayson said.

I looked at the screen and saw I assumed wrong.

"My bad," I replied.

"Well, who was you boutta scream at? That fuckboy, Derrick, I saw calling you last night?" He sounded jealous.

"Could have been," I played with him.

"Baby girl, stop. I'm glad you liked the dress and shoes. You got it on now?" he asked in a suggestive tone.

"Maybe," I said, picking up two thick ass T-bone steaks.

"Can I get a picture?" he asked.

"No. What, you think we cool now?" I smiled as I talked.

"Yeah, I see you answered and your voice wasn't like it was before. You was happy to hear from a nigga, wasn't you?" I could hear his police radio going off in the background.

"Well, I guess you got niggas to lock up and shit, right?" I grabbed some Simply Lemonade.

"Yup, starting with your ass. Let me use the cuffs on you one time."

"Your ass only think about sex, I see." I shook my head.

"No, I just know what I want."

"You got that 25?" I laughed into the phone.

"Stop playin' with me, Kola, before I fuck your ass up. I played your game because the shit was cute, baby, but that shit is dead."

"Yeah, we will see when you think you gonna get some pussy." I rolled my eyes at the broad who was all in my mouth.

"I bet you ask me to fuck you before I ask your ass, since we playin' around and shit."

"Yeah, whatever. I gotta go, bye." I slid my phone into my bra and picked up everything I needed to make a steak dinner to say thank you. I wasn't a total bitch, it was the least I could do.

I paid for everything and headed back to Jayson's house, playing around with the Lambo a little bit before pulling into his driveway. I let myself in with the keys and set the bags down. I didn't know what time he came home, but it was already into the evening, and I wanted to at least have something cooking before I checked to see where he was.

I put a 30-minute Grill Mates marinade on the steaks in a zip lock bag, then went to chill for a minute. After pouring myself an icy ass glass of lemonade, I chilled and waited for the steaks. I wanted to be nosey and go through his shit, but instead, I texted Shay and watched some TV until I was ready to throw the steaks on. I had an idea, but since I didn't know what time he came home, it might be useless. I did it anyway, though.

I started cooking and turned on some music, then stripped ass naked and put the heels back on. I giggled at the thought of him catching me in my birthday suit cooking in his kitchen. Minutes later, I hear the door close. I smiled and didn't turn around when I heard the footsteps approaching.

"Eeeeew, what the fuck," I heard a female voice behind me say.

I turned around and saw the broad who had come down the steps that day I came over. I quickly grabbed my dress and covered up.

"What the fuck is right. Why you walkin' up in here and shit?" I asked and gritted on her.

"The door was unlocked, and I came to talk to Jay, but I find your fat ass in here trying to play house."

"Oh, bitch, all this thickness is shittin' on your ass. Ask Jay, hoe." I smirked and cocked my head to the side.

"Who would want some fat bitch smushing them all the time?" She started laughing.

"A nigga like me."

I heard Jay voice but didn't see him yet. He walked around the corner, and his mouth dropped.

"You playin'." He walked up and pushed his tongue into my mouth. "You cookin' for a nigga and shit, ass naked. And you got the heels I bought you on." He stepped back and yanked the dress I was holding in front of me away.

"Really, Jay? You never got me shit!" the girl yelled.

I almost forgot she was there.

"Exactly. That should tell your ass something. Why you even here?" he asked and wrapped his arms around me as he stared into my eyes.

"Keep the fat hoe, then. You ain't gotta worry about me."

She was asking for this ass whopping.

"I rather my bitch have some meat. She badder than you, hoe. Get the fuck on, and if you show up at my house again, I won't be a sweetheart about the shit." He pulled his gun out and laid it on the counter.

I heard the food sizzling and remembered what I was doing.

"Go to hell, Jay." She left, and he kept his attention on me.

"So, damn. I thought I was the enemy, and you gave me a gift like this." He stepped back and smacked my ass, then watched it jiggle.

"Mmmm, it was more like a thank you."

I took the steaks out one by one, and laid them on the plates. I scooped up the peppers and onions I fried and laid them on top. I felt the first kiss land on my right shoulder, and it sent a shuddering sensation down my spine.

"Ssss, I thought I would be asking to fuck first," I said, enjoying the kisses he trailed down my side to my hip bone.

"Who said we was fuckin'?" He stopped and kissed me roughly.

"I'ma go get ready to eat."

He looked down at my titties and grabbed his dick. This nigga had my pussy ready, but I knew I wasn't giving in to his ass that easily.

Jayson

I quickly changed so I could get back downstairs to Kola's sexy ass. She was right, I almost fucked her, but I caught myself. I didn't think she would still be there after this morning, but there she was. I knew she had feelings for a nigga, otherwise, why would she go through all the trouble? I liked how she seemed a little more feminine than before. It made her even more attractive to me.

When I got back to the kitchen, Kola was gone. I went to the dining room and found her sitting in front of her plate. Damn, this shit looked good as a motherfucker.

"I'm boutta fuck this shit up." I grabbed the A-1 and opened it.

"Yeah, I'm hungry as hell," she said and scooped up her potatoes.

"So, why you decided to stay?" I asked, curious as hell.

"I don't know, I really don't." She shook her head.

"I do. It eats you up that you feelin' a nigga, don't it?"

"Oh, shut up. You swear you know what you talkin' about," she snapped.

I jumped up and grabbed her by her cheeks then kissed her lips.

"Your lips for kissin', not talkin' shit to me." I kissed her again and let her go.

I could help but be drawn to that sexy ass naked body she had laid out for a nigga.

"You droolin'." She snapped me out of my zone.

We continued to eat dinner, and all I could think about was ripping her ass apart. But, I had already made it clear that she was gonna want me first, so I had to hold on until I could get her ready to break down for the dick.

"Can you drop me off at my spot on Beach later?" She asked as she put on the dress I bought her.

"I thought you was done with all that shit, and why don't you spend the night?" I asked.

"Uh, no. I still need to make money," she said.

"Nah, you don't need to do that shit," I said, drinking my beer.

"Nigga, you still ain't offer me no coin. I gotta keep grinding, so..." She rolled her eyes.

"Then stop being stupid and give a nigga a real chance to show you I'm more than my badge." I got up and pulled the dress back off.

"What are you doing?" she asked as I slid a finger between her pussy lips.

"You don't like to cum?" I asked and licked her neck. I could feel her shiver. Those pretty ass chocolate nipples stood at attention, and I kissed the left one first.

"Stop," she said, surprising me by pulling away. "I can't do this, I don't even know what I'm doin'. You make me feel some type of way. I ain't felt this shit in a long time, but you the wrong nigga, Jay." For some reason, she looked like she was about to cry.

"How the fuck am I the wrong nigga? Ain't no nigga put you in heels or made you switch up that I'm a tough bitch routine. How many niggas you cooked for, baby girl? You pushed me away, and even tried to extort a nigga. Maybe them other niggas was the wrong nigga. Fuck it, I give up. You can go. You ain't ready for a nigga like me, sweetheart."

I gritted, getting pissed because she was on too much bullshit for me. I ain't chase no fucking body except her, and she too fucking blind to see when a nigga likes her ass.

"Okay, cool then, Jay. You probably couldn't handle a bitch like me anyway." She chuckled, and that shit pissed me off.

"Go the fuck upstairs, get in the bed, and that shit better be off." I walked past her and went to the closet to pull my work bag out.

"Jay—"

"What the fuck I say, Kola? Why you still standing here?" I barked, causing her to jump.

She went up the stairs, and I followed. She needed to understand who the fuck she was dealing with. By the time I'm done with her tonight, she gon' be sucking her thumb in the fucking corner.

"So, you asking for pussy like you said you wasn't?" she said, still playing games.

"I ain't asking for shit."

I got on the bed, where she did exactly what I told her. She was naked again, and her body looked like art. I put the hand cuffs on her quickly before she could protest and cuffed her to the bed.

"What the hell are you doin'?" she yelled but quickly shut up when I eased my dick into her mouth.

"See, your problem is you talk too much."

I grabbed her head and pushed in and out of her mouth. I had her submissive as fuck because she was sucking it like she meant it. I pulled it out her mouth and went to slide into her pussy.

"Fuck me." She moaned as I put the head in.

"You sure?" I teased her.

"Please." She moaned while I started to circle her clit with my dick.

"Nah, you need to be calmed down, and if I give you dick, it's just gonna get worse."

I kissed inside her thighs, and I could smell her pussy scent. It drove me crazy. I kissed it first before I dove in.

"Shit, Jay."

She arched her back, and I heard the cuffs as she tried to move her hands. I could tell by how she was bouncing that she was about to cum, so I stopped and laid next to her.

"What the fuck, Jay?" she whined.

I chuckled and went down to the kitchen to grab some ice. I was gonna torture her body all night, and not give her no dick. She would be begging me when I'm done. I put a piece of ice in my mouth before I got in the room. She had her body twisted, and the shit was picture perfect. I took my baton out my bag and traced it over her nipples, down to her pussy.

"Jay." She gasped as I slid the tip up and down her clit.

"I knew you would like the shit," I said and smiled after taking the ice out my mouth.

I dropped the baton and started at her feet. I popped the ice back into my mouth and traced her body with it, and she was going crazy as fuck off it.

"Please, just fuck me," she said and opened her legs. I was so tempted after seeing the wet spot I created under her.

"No, if I can't keep my word to you, how you gonna trust me in the future?" I smirked, enjoying this shit.

"I hate you." She kicked at me, and I grabbed her foot.

"No, you don't." I pushed her legs apart and went right back to licking up her pussy.

"Shiiiit!" she screamed when I opened her ass cheeks and slipped my tongue into her ass.

I felt her lock up, and I knew I was on my job. I fucked with her body all night before letting her out the cuffs. She was past pissed because I didn't slip her no dick.

We continued to go back and forth for weeks, until one day she popped up on a nigga when I was chillin' with my peoples and shit. She was pissed that I hadn't called her in a few days. The text she sent earlier said it all.

I was talking to Missile and Tadah when I saw her thick ass walking toward me.

"Really?" She smacked her teeth and pushed me.

I knew she was crazy about not getting no dick. I had been eating pussy and even ass, but I ain't slide in that shit.

"I was chillin', bae. I was gonna hit you back." I reached for her hand.

"Yeah, whatever." She waved me off.

"You pullin' up on a nigga, bae?" I smiled and leaned against the car as I drank out my cup.

"Nigga, you play all fuckin' day. I know you saw me callin' your ass."

I could hear my niggas snickering and shit.

"Damn, lil mama, chill the fuck out. What's so important?" I grabbed her up, and she tried to fight, but I had a hold on her ass.

"Get off me, nigga. I just came to tell your ass that I wasn't fuckin' with you." She got free and walked off. I went behind her and threw my arm around her neck.

"So instead of not fuckin' with me, you came to tell me you not fuckin' with me?" I chuckled.

"I can't stand you, nigga. And fuck you," she said and flipping the bird to my friends, who all raised their brows. She was fierce.

"I hurt your feelings not callin'?" I kissed her on the side of her cheek.

"No, I didn't care, but—"

"You wanna be with me or not? You can't expect boyfriend shit and not wanna be my girl. So, I mean, wassup?"

"I don't know, damn."

"Then call me when you do know. I don't wanna just fuck you, even though that pussy fiyah. I want you to be my heart-beat, you hear me? So holla at me when we on that type of shit." I kissed her and walked back over to my homies.

Kola got in her car and left. I was distracted the rest of the night because now I just wanted to be with Kola. I went ahead and sent her some flowers and went back to chillin'.

Kola

I can't believe I pulled up on that nigga. I felt like a thirsty bitch just as I was when I went looking for Anthony that day. I still missed him so much, and now I felt like maybe I was scared to have somebody really take his place and have my heart again.

That's why I was standing at his grave with a smile, thinking of our days over and over again. I lay down and touched his tombstone.

"I don't wanna let you go, baby. You was everything, nigga. Every fuckin' thing, I swear. I remember the last time we made love, and I can still feel it sometimes. How you had me spread open on our dining room table. You told me you loved me so many times, baby, and I told you the same. I still love you. We were supposed to be old and shit together, fighting and talkin' shit to each other while our grandkids laughed.

"Don't be mad, but I like this guy. He reminds me of you sometimes, always willing to do anything to make me smile. I want to be with him, Anthony." I stopped talking when I saw a flock of ducks walk by, and one had a flower in its mouth.

He walked right up to me and dropped it in my lap, and then walked off. I picked it up and started crying.

"I love you too, baby." I kissed his headstone and walked away.

I texted Jayson.

Me: *We on that type of shit now.*

Jay: Oh yeah, come holla at your nigga then.

I smiled and looked back at Anthony's grave.

"Thank you," I said.

I got in my car and went to see my nigga.

*****

"Derrick, I told you it's cool. We good, aight?" I said to him as he talked in my phone, trying to slide through.

"Aight, Kola." He hung up.

"You need to let that nigga know you got a man before I smoke his ass," Jay said, walking in and handing me a blunt.

"I did. Didn't you just hear me?" I rolled my eyes.

"You need to watch that attitude." He kissed me and bit my bottom lip.

"The fuck." I pushed his shoulder.

"Get ready and stop whining." He pinched my ass.

"Watch where I bite you," I said and looked down at his dick.

I turned the shower on and got in. I loved my Dove Ultra-moisture because it had my skin feeling sexy as fuck.

Jay opened the bathroom door and tried to join me, but I held the glass door closed.

"Stop playin'." He tried to pull it.

"No, you bit me," I teased.

"Aight, you gon be usin' a dildo to fuck if you don't let me in," he threatened.

I stomped my foot and let go.

"I thought so." He immediately covered my lips with his and rubbed up and down my soapy ass.

"Shit." I broke our kiss once he started teasing my pussy with his dick.

"I ain't gotta ask you if this my pussy." He lifted my leg and slid deep into me.

I gasped as his dick filled me up. He wasn't even all the way inside.

"Fuck, baby." I clenched my eyes as he slowly grinded into me. He had me hiccupping when he sped up.

"Damn, bitch."

Jayson put my leg down and bent me over. He pulled both arms behind my back and put that monster back in my pussy. He had me at his mercy with those back shots. My legs started to shake as I felt my first nut hit my pussy.

"Shit." He pulled out and came on the shower floor.

"Damn, I ain't wanna cum, but shit." He smacked my ass.

"That's cool, I think I would have died if I took any more." I laughed.

"Well, when we get back from this move, I'ma see if I can kill you with some death strokes." His ass was so simple.

I was kind of nervous because Jayson asked me to meet his family. I thought it was kind of soon, but it made me feel like he was serious about us committing. We got in the car looking like a sexy ass hood couple. We were cute, I couldn't front.

I took a breath as we got out. I didn't give a fuck If they liked me, but I knew it would be smoother If they did.

"You look sexy as fuck." Jay said as he got out the car and looked at my ass. The door opened before we got to it, and a nice looking older lady came out and smiled at us.

"Wow, a dark chocolate beauty. Lord, I'm jealous." She raised her arms for me to hug her.

I hugged her and Jay hugged her when I pulled back.

As soon as we were going in, Jay's phone rang.

"Fuck." He walked down the steps and took his call on the curb.

"So, what's your name? You ain't just another bitch who want his money, are you?" his mother came straight out of nowhere.

"What the fuck you just say to me?"

"Bae..." Jay called out to me.

I scowled at his mother and walked to him.

"Your mother just said some wild shit." I used my thumb to point behind my back.

"Her ass is crazy, don't trip. Look, I gotta go. I got a case," he said, looking somewhat embarrassed.

"Me or the pigs," I said and folded my arms.

He leaned back and looked at me.

"You heard me, Jay." I looked at him seriously.

"Say you my bitch forever, and I'll turn the papers in." He stroked my legs.

"You have to want me because you want me, Jay, not just the idea of me. You ready to settle down, right?" I said, meaning every word.

119

"Yeah, I am," he answered.

"If you're sure, then we can see how it goes, Jay. We didn't start off too good." I giggled.

"It's about how we finish." He kissed me.

He dropped me off and promised to be back as soon as possible. I couldn't wait for him to come back.

As soon as I heard that doorbell after a few hours, I ran my ass to the door. I swung the door open and jumped on him, and then locked hands with him and let him carry me upstairs.

We made some good love all fucking night. Jay and Kola, I always thought it had a ring to it.

Now that you have me, motherfucker you don't know how to treat me...

Jayson

2 years later

"Fuck, Kola, this pussy wet as fuck!"

I swear, I can't get enough of her ass. It had been two years since I got Kola to be on my team, and a nigga couldn't be happier. She definitely matched my fly. She was still in the game, but as my right hand. If I could have it my way, she wouldn't even be doing that, but her ass is stubborn as fuck, so I let her work closely with me.

"Yes, daddy, hit the shit!" She moaned as I hit it from the back.

I watched her fat ass jiggle and smiled.

"Shit, girl, I'm 'bout to cum!"

She threw that ass back, and before I knew it, I had busted all in her, hoping to get her pregnant. Shit, I had been trying for the past year, and that shit still ain't happened.

"Nigga, that was bomb. Now I need a nap." She laid on the bed and smiled at me.

"I gotta make a few runs today, but after that, I wanna go out. We ain't did shit in a minute," I told her as I walked into the bathroom that was attached to our room.

Life had been good since I left the force. It's been two years, and I can't say I'm mad about it. I mean, it sucks not knowing inside details, but it is what it is.

"So, nigga, when are we gonna make this shit official and get married?"

Here she go with that shit again. I loved Kola and I was definitely marrying her, but not on her time. I wish she would just let that shit go because I already had shit in the works, but she was fucking nagging me.

"Not now, Kola!" I flushed the toilet and walked out the bathroom. A Nigga couldn't even shit in peace.

"Then when, Jay? I mean, you practically made me your bitch against my will, and now you don't want to commit to me!"

"Against your will? Nah, baby, you was feeling the kid. But if you don't want this anymore, leave!"

She pouted, but I didn't give a fuck. She was starting to get on my damn nerves.

"You a straight asshole, my nigga!" She stomped away, but that shit didn't faze me. I was used to Kola's tantrums. It was partially my fault because I spoiled her ass all the time.

I went to the closet and grabbed my clothes for the day and

headed to the shower. Hopefully by the time I got back, she'd be out of her feelings.

***

"Damn, Jay, where you been hiding?"

I looked over to my right and saw Ashley. I hadn't seen her in a while until a few months ago when she started working at this spot. I couldn't help but think about the bitch having a mean head game. I think she was missing her tonsils.

"What up, Ash?" I nodded.

I was at the strip club with my boy, Aaron. Aaron was my other right hand next to Kola. I had been hustling with Aaron since we were youngins but I was just now putting him on. He had done a bid like a lot of my niggas from back in the day.

"Damn, that's all I get? You must be fucking with one of those bourgeois bitches you be meeting." She rolled her eyes.

"Nah, my bitch ain't bougie, but she will fuck you up. So, if I was you, I would keep it moving lil ma."

She rolled her eyes again before walking away.

"Damn, bruh, Kola ass got you sprung if you turning down Ashley."

"Hell yeah. I love her spoiled ass, plus I ain't trying to have her shooting me and shit. Her lil mean ass a pull a gun in a minute, and not give a fuck."

We laughed.

"Damn, bruh, tell her to hook me up with her friend," Aaron said as he grabbed his drink from the waitress.

"I'll tell her."

It was a little after ten. I knew Kola was going be pissed at me because I was supposed to have gone back home and took her out, but I got sidetracked fucking with this nigga!

"Aye, man, I'm about to head out before you be attending my funeral," I joked seriously.

"Aight, man, I'll holla!"

I headed out the door and home to my baby. I just hoped she wasn't too pissed because I needed some pussy.

"Jay." Aaron ran up and grabbed my shoulder.

"Wassup?"

He shook his head before speaking. "You ain't going home right now, bruh. You need to go talk to your brother. He ain't tell you the connect got lost?"

"Wait, what the fuck you mean? I just talked to Ruiz."

"Well, he got into it with some of his folks when he went to pick up a lil sum, and your brother flipped out and told him y'all didn't need 'em."

"Man, he did what? What the fuck." I stomped out and hit Kola to let her know what was up.

Me: *I'ma be home bae, I gotta be a stupid motherfucker.*

Kola: *Its cool bae, I'ma put your food in the microwave.*

See, that's my bitch.

I called to see where Duane was, and this nigga didn't answer the phone.

He called back, though.

"Bruh, fuck is you at?" I asked his dumb ass.

"It wasn't all me, Jay. That nigga tested us like we was weak, man."

"I don't give a fuck, Duane. I ain't talking about this shit over the phone." I hung up and headed to his house. He could be so stupid some fucking times.

I told Aaron I would holla at him later and drove straight over to Duane's. I banged on the door but heard commotion inside, so I turned the knob, and it happened to be open. This nigga was slipping like shit. I heard screams coming from the living room and saw Duane beating Tiffany's ass. I ran over and pushed him off her.

"Nigga, what the fuck is you doin', cuh?" I said as I helped her up.

"You don't tell me how to handle my bitch, Jay. That hoe keep tryin' me, and I'ma keep givin' her what she want." He walked up, looking just like the nigga who played biggie in the movie.

"Nah, not in front of me, nigga. I'm already on a thousand, nigga," I said.

"Bitch, get the fuck upstairs. I swear, if you try to pack a bag, I'm goin' hard," Duane said, looking at me, but talking to Tiffany.

"I wanna leave, Jay. Help me." She grabbed my arm.

Duane started to run toward her, but I stood between them.

"I ain't here for this shit. You fucked our connect up with your dumb ass attitude, nigga. Now, I gotta make shit right. I ain't sendin' you or those bitch ass niggas you run with. I don't know what the fuck your new problems about, but that shit needs to be fixed. I ain't losing shit, you hear me? So, fix that shit, cuz I'm at a point where I'm startin' not to give a fuck about the blood we share."

"Don't threaten me."

"It's a fact. Oh, and Ma's birthday coming up so, act like a son and be at her party."

I walked out, not giving a fuck about his feelings. That nigga wasn't right, and I could feel it.

****

"I got them Versace t-shirts for the low."

"iPhone 7 for 200."

The boosters were out in full force as I fought through them to get to this jewelry store for my baby. I wanted to make sure the ring I ordered her was perfect before I proposed. When I walked in, the bitches who worked there all put their titties up and smiles on.

"Hey, Jay. Came to worry us about your ring?" Selena smiled and leaned over the counter.

"You know it. Did y'all add what I needed?" I asked.

I got the inside inscribed to say

My forever and always, love Jay

"It's not back yet. I don't know what's going on with our people, but they been slower than usual." She shrugged.

"Man, what the fuck? Look, tell them mufuckas to hurry up. Y'all boutta run my money back." I took out my phone when I felt it vibrating in my pocket.

"Baby, you ready for tonight?" I asked Kola when I saw that it was her calling.

"Yeees, I went and got a new outfit and everything. I been excited since this morning. I hope we going to the steak house," she said all fast.

"We can go wherever you want, baby girl."

I walked out the jewelry store after watching the envy on the sales girls' faces as I spoke to Kola.

"What time you coming, so I can be ready?"

"I'll be there at like 8, aight? I got to go on this lil drive real fast," I said in code.

I was letting her know that I had to go talk to a few of my customers. I looked at the time and saw that it was 4:00 already. I had to hurry up because with traffic, the drive was gonna be stupid. I sat in that deadlocked bullshit and finally made it to the first place on Avalon.

I parked a block away and walked down to the orange and blue house at the end of the street.

"Wassup, Jay?" A lil nigga who runs for Loco nodded.

"Sup."

I walked past him and the rest of them niggas who were out there and walked up to knock on the door.

"Jay, wassup, man?" Loco opened the door all the way and let me in.

"You know wassup, nigga. You told Duane you needed to be fronted, and then you don't even have the money for the last shipment. I ain't welfare, nigga." I sat on the arm of the couch.

"I know, Jay, but you know we got hit, and—"

"Nah, you ain't get hit. I took my shit back. I heard you was fuckin' with some Muslims. Trying to buy shit off them, and short me." I pulled out my strap, and his nigga ran up, but I busted his ass in the face.

"For real, nigga? You think I'm stupid enough to fuck with you, bruh?" he said, sounding nervous.

"I do."

I kicked him away from me and shot him in the head. I didn't want any blood to get on me.

I opened the door, and all the niggas outside had their heads down as I walked past. They already knew.

I got in the car and headed toward Q's ass because he said he came across a nigga trying to cut me off and shit. I got to Q's house and jumped out to see what the fuck he was talking about real quick.

I knocked and he opened it like he was waiting.

"My nigga," he said and dapped me up with a weird ass look on his face.

"Nigga who else here?" I asked and pulled my gun out.

"Damn, still ready to shoot any and everybody." I heard a voice that I knew must have been a mistake.

"Aye, get the fuck outta here! My nigga Colby on the street," I said, going up and hugging him.

Colby was my homie from so far back. I can't even remember how long. This nigga dropped a nigga who tried to drop me and got caught. I owed this nigga.

"We gotta pop a bottle, my nigga. How the fuck you get out?" I asked and sat on the couch."

"My lawyer got my shit overturned on some technical shit."

"I already got bottles, my nigga." Q sat some Jack Daniels on the table.

"To my nigga fuckin' up some blocks." I grabbed a glass and poured up.

I looked at the phone and saw that I still had some time before getting Kola, so I kicked it and got bent.

Kola

"Really, Jay? I thought you were taking me out." I met Jay at the door, dressed in a 2000 dollar outfit, and I had nowhere to go. I was beyond pissed at this fool.

"My bad, bae, I got caught up," he had the nerve to say.

He kissed me on the cheek, smelling like liquor, and walked his ass to the steps.

"Whatever. Fuck you, nigga!"

Before he could respond, I picked up the plant that was sitting on the table in the foyer and threw it at his damn head.

I could hear him cursing as I ran my ass to the basement and locked myself in the bathroom. I needed to learn to control my temper, and now I knew I had probably pissed him off. I could hear the loud thuds of his shoes as they came down the steps. I turned the light off like that would make a difference. He knew exactly where I was.

"Kola, open this fuckin' door!"

"No! I hate your ass!" I said and hit the door.

He got quiet, and I assumed he left. The first kick at the door, I saw the hinges shake.

"You stay thinking I'm playing with your ass, Kola!" he said before kicking again and sending the door flying off the hinge.

He stood at the door with his shirt off, showing all of the tattoos that covered his arms and chest. He rushed to me, snatching my lil ass up and pulling me out the bathroom. I started hit him in his arms, and he didn't seem fazed by it.

"Get off me!" I said and yanked away so hard I fell.

He started laughing, which pissed me off even further.

"Stop acting fuckin' stupid, Kola. I don't feel like one of your crazy sessions and shit." He grabbed me and started pulling me up the steps.

"Clean this shit up and bring your ass upstairs." He kissed my cheek and headed up.

I went to the kitchen and got the broom and dust pain. He still wasn't getting off easy. I hated when we made plans and he always got fucking caught up. I cleaned up the mess I made and headed up to make this nigga listen.

When I got upstairs, he was knocked out on the bed without a care in the world. I just changed my clothes and went into the guest bedroom and laid down. I didn't give a fuck how mad he would be in the morning that I didn't wake up with him. He thought he was going to stand me up like some ugly prom date, and I was tired of that shit.

******

The next morning, I woke up to Jay lying across me and snoring. I started to push him, and he got up and laid on the pillow. He just couldn't sleep without me for shit. I got up, only to be pulled back down.

"Where you going?" Jayson asked.

"Wherever the hell I want, as long as it's away from your ass," I said.

"Kola, cut the shit, man. I said I was sorry about last night.

I promise, tonight we can go where you want." He kissed me on the hand.

"Aight Jay, whatever you say."

I wasn't moved, I knew something would happen where I would be alone again like last night.

"I promise, bae."

He got up and kissed me on the collar bone. I didn't want to smile, but it just crept across my face easily when he did that. I knew he was ready to fuck, but I wanted to teach his ass a little lesson. I pulled myself away and got up, leaving his ass sitting on the bed looking dumbfounded, just like he left me last night.

I grabbed my phone from our room and checked a few messages and read some texts. One of them was from Sammi. I didn't know why this mufucka insisted on texting me incriminating shit. I called him, and he answered right away.

"Nigga, you mildly retarded or some shit? When you need to talk, you hit me. Don't do that shit no more," I said in a serious tone.

"My bad, I was just—"

"Don't really give a fuck, nigga. Now where the fuck was the problem?" I asked, referring to the corner that got robbed yesterday.

"Florence. Marco said some Vegas niggas been coming through asking questions and shit. He thinks it was them," he said.

"Aight."

I hung up and turned around to see Jayson leaned against the wall. I rolled my eyes and went to pick out some clothes for the day. I needed to go holla at these fools so we could handle some business.

"Kola," Jay called me, but I kept searching through my clothes.

"I know your ass hear me talking to you." He came through the door of my walk-in closet.

"My bad, aight." He kissed my forehead.

"Yeah, I know, Jay." I pulled down a baby tee and buttoned my jumper.

"Look, I said I was sorry, aight. That shit dead, and I ain't trying to keep fighting about the same shit. Now what was that about on the phone?" he asked skipping into business mode.

"We got hit. I'm going to see about the shit now." I grabbed my towel off the back of the closet door.

He pulled me close and shoved his tongue in my mouth.

"Handle that shit." He smacked my ass and headed out the closet.

I got showered and dressed, and when I got out, Jay had some breakfast sitting on the bed from Carl's Jr for me. I smiled and ate after I got dressed.

I made my moves and found out them Vegas niggas been moving around and shit. They left a trail, and I knew where I could find their ass. Jay wouldn't let me go, of course, so he told me to just send some fools and be done with the shit. I didn't understand what the point of me working was if I couldn't do shit. I mean, I've been asking him about marriage and shit too. He wanted me to be a wife and just lay back and chill, but he didn't want to make me a wife.

I wish I could tell him the real reason I was scared to have a baby. I was afraid I would lose him and the baby like what happened with Anthony. I was hoping that if we got married first and did it in a different order my results would be different. I know it sounds dumb, but I can't handle any more losses. I loved him, but he needed to make a real commitment. I gave up my whole life for him, and now he needed to do the same for me.

Jayson

I had to find a way to make up for missing our date. Kola was my heart, and I went through too much to get her just to lose her. That shit wasn't happening. I had to start doing better because she wasn't some basic bitch. She kept pressuring me to marry her ass, but what she didn't know was that shit was a done deal. I just wanted this shit to be perfect, so I had to come correct because she deserved the best.

Baby girl was leaving for Miami with her girls next month, and I was planning to surprise her while she was there. Shit, it was time. We had more money than we knew what to do with, and we weren't getting any younger. I was ready for marriage and kids.

I was still feeling the effects of the liquor, so I laid my ass down to sleep it off. Tomorrow, I had to go look at a few houses for Kola, and I needed to be on my A game.

*****

Kola was up early on a Saturday to get on my damn nerves. I was lying in bed trying to get some damn sleep, but she was running around trying to clean up. Looking at the clock on the nightstand pissed me off even more because it was 8:00 in the damn morning, and like I said, it was fucking Saturday.

"Kola, please lay the fuck down and shut the hell up." I covered my face with the pillow.

"Ughh. Whatever." She got in the bed and laid down.

I turned over and threw my arm over her. "When we get up, we can go get you some food so you can be nice to a nigga."

She laughed after I said that. I was able to go back to sleep for a little while, but when I woke up, Kola was eating a big ass sandwich and watching TV.

"Welcome back," she said and put the sandwich to my mouth.

I bit it and laid back down.

"What time is it?" I asked, not feeling like turning toward the clock.

"Two." She looked at me and threw my phone in my lap.

"Your phone been blowing up. Some blocked number." She cut her eyes at me.

"It's prolly that nigga who keep crying that he's my father." I unlocked my phone and saw that he had texted again.

Kola was all in the screen.

"You happy?" I asked, holding the phone closer to her.

He had asked to see me again.

"Well, why don't you see what he wants?"

"I don't need to see that bitch ass nigga. Fuck him." I put the phone on the nightstand and felt my stomach growl.

"Let's go get some food." I got out of bed and stretched.

"Aight, but I wanted to wait until you fully woke up to tell you that Q called too."

I could tell the shit wasn't good by the look on her face.

"Well, wassup?" I asked, irritated that if it was real shit, the first thing out her mouth was about a blocked number calling me.

"He said he wanted to holla at us. Said it was about some lost chickens." She knew I was about to go off.

"Come on, bring that ass in the shower. I need some pussy before I hear this shit." I took my underwear off and threw it in the clothes bin.

"No. You ain't gonna hurt me cuz you mad."

She took her shorts and t-shirt off and tried to walk by like she wasn't about to get that pussy banged out.

As soon we got in the bathroom, I bent her over the sink and slid up in that wet pussy. I knew she wanted some dick, and this slippery shit was life right now.

"Damn, bitch." I looked down at my baby's chocolate ass and stopped to bite that motherfucker.

She yelped, and that shit excited me. I slapped her ass hard and slid back inside. I wanted to suck on some titties, so I turned her around and put her up on the counter. I pulled that pretty ass nipple in my mouth and watch Kola squirm in the mirror.

I cuffed her legs and slid my dick right back up in the pussy.

"Damn, I feel this shit in my toes." Kola wrapped her legs around me and pulled me closer.

I loved the sound of my dick pumping in and out of her pussy.

"Fuck, cum on the dick now." I grabbed her throat and pushed deep. I hit her with short strokes, banging that spot every time.

I saw her eyes and roll in the back of her head, and then she threw her head back with her mouth wide open. Her big titties bounced, and she bounced on the counter and did as I told her.

I didn't last much longer after I felt that pussy cup my dick. I loved, Kola's ass, but that pussy would have been enough to make a nigga stay right there. She had that special deluxe, keep a nigga stuck on dumb pussy.

When I drained all I could from my balls, I called Duane to see what was up with Aaron. I got a crazy call last night from him, but I couldn't hear shit he said. I just knew Duane had met up with him last night.

"Aye. You talk to Aaron?" I asked him as soon as he picked up.

"Yeah, but he ain't never show up last night." He yawned.

"What the fuck?" My other line beeped, and I saw Sammi calling. Hopefully, he'd heard from Aaron.

"Lemme hit you back." I hung up on Duane.

"What's good, nigga? You heard from Aaron?" I quickly asked.

"My nigga," he said. "It's crazy you asked that. They found that nigga's body this morning, cuh. Charmaine, Truck's lil sister told me. Shot that man like twenty times"

I closed my eyes and shook my head. I lost had lost niggas before, and each time was fucked up.

"Find out who did that shit," I said and hung up.

"What's wrong?" Kola asked, coming up to me.

"Aaron got murked." I sat on the bed and took a deep breath.

"Baby, I'm sorry." She sat on the bed stroking my dreads.

"It's cool. That's why I need me a son, bae. I need somebody to carry on when I die."

"You ain't dying, I won't let you." She giggled.

I smiled because I knew she was serious.

"I love you, bae." I kissed her and got ready to go be ignorant on these motherfuckers.

Kola and I got dressed then went straight to Sammi to see what was up. He said he already had people talking. When I pulled up to him, I saw Duane leaning on the fence without a care in the world.

"Oh, so we ain't got shit to do, huh?" I said, getting out and opening the door for Kola.

"We was wai—"

"I don't give a fuck if you was waiting on Jesus to come back, mufucka. Y'all got me fucked up," I said, looking at Sammi and Duane.

"Chill, bro, niggas die every day, B," Duane said and cracked a dumb ass smile.

"Oh yeah, shit funny, right?" I swung and hit him right across the jaw, and we started fighting.

"Jay!" Kola called out, but I couldn't stop.

"Bitch ass nigga," Duane said, pushing me off then breathing heavily.

"You a fuck nigga. Get the fuck outta here before I kill my own blood," I told him and pulled my strap.

"It's like that, Jay?" He nodded and spit out blood.

"Bae—" Kola started.

"Nigga, do it." Duane cut her off.

"Bae, just—"

"Bitch, what? You don't fuckin' see me talkin'? Go get in the fuckin' car, damn." I barked at her and immediately regretted calling her a bitch.

Before I could blink, Kola caught my ass with a nice one to the jaw.

"Fuck you." She walked off quicker than I could catch her and apologize.

One of my good men just got laid out, and I was pissed at Duane. I shouldn't have taken it out on her. I let Sammi go talk to the niggas, and I went to find her. She got low quick as shit.

I called her phone and got no answer.

I called again, and this time it picked up.

"Hello."

I didn't recognize the voice. "Who the fuck is this?"

"This is Shay, Kola said if she a bitch then call a non bitch." And the hoe hung up.

Childish as fuck.

****

I woke up the next day to an empty bed. That didn't sit well with me, so I grabbed my phone and called Kola's ass.

"What, Jay?" she answered, and that shit further pissed me off.

"Where the fuck are you?" I yelled.

"In my skin!"

That was one thing I couldn't get used to, her smart ass mouth.

"Don't fucking play with me! Where the fuck are you?"

"Look, Jay, I just needed a day to myself."

"So, you spend the night out? Where the fuck they do that shit?"

"Look, I'll be home in a few, and then we can talk unless I'm still a bitch," she replied, but it wasn't that fucking simple.

"Nah, I'm about to go." I hung up and got up to get my day started.

Her little ass had me all the way fucked up, but she was gon' learn today. I made my way to the bathroom to shower so I could get the fuck out the house before Kola got there. I really wasn't trying to fuck with her ass today. I turned the water on as hot as I could get it and got in. I was about to show her little ass that she could play the game all she wanted, but I invented this shit.

When I got out the shower, Kola was sitting on the bed, but I wasn't fucking with her ass. I went to the closet and grabbed me some clothes. I decided to keep it simple with a pair of black Levi's and a white tee. I had some new Balmain boots that I wanted to break out. Them bitches was dope as fuck, not to mention I spent a grip on them.

"So, you really gon' move around like I'm not here, Jay?"

I ignored her ass because she was in deep shit with me. I didn't play that disrespectful shit, and her not coming home last night was beyond disrespectful.

"Jay?" she called out, but I just kept doing me.

I sprayed on some Gucci Guilty then grabbed my Falcons snap back and my Cartier watch. After checking my appearance in the mirror, I headed out the room, and of course, she was on my heels. As I reached the door, I felt her ass grab my arm.

"What, Kola? You weren't trying to talk when yo ass stayed out all night." I gave her a menacing stare because I was indeed pissed.

"I needed time, Jay!"

"Time from what? I give you every fucking thing! I'm out here risking my ass so you can drive foreign cars and take trips internationally and shit! I do what I do so you can live good and not have to hustle and run hoe houses, but you needed space! Fuck you, Kola!" I walked out the door even more pissed off.

I couldn't believe she had the nerve to let that shit come out her mouth. Then I gotta deal with her ass nagging me about marrying her instead of being patient and letting me be a man about mine. She was really making me regret chasing her ass. Something had to give because I dint know how much more I could deal with. I loved her ass, but she needed to get her shit together before she becomes single for a minute.

***

A few weeks later

"You took jewels off my bitch's fingers. You ain't think I would miss two little ole keys and shit, huh?" I talked to lil Nick, who was one of my stash house lieutenants in San Francisco.

Yeah, I took a jet with a few of my niggas to tune these mufuckas up. I didn't give a fuck where I was, a nigga was gonna get reached.

"You got this shit fucked up, man. I swear, everything was there, Jay," he said with a look in his eyes that let me know this nigga wasn't lying.

If he didn't steal my shit, then who did? Had to be a nigga who was in the stash all the time.

"Well, who got the shit, then? Because we don't. So, I guess I'ma cut off each finger until you got some words, my nigga." I snipped off his pinky finger with the gardening shears.

He screamed and threw up immediately.

"It was probably J-Rock, man. You got to believe meeee." He broke down crying.

"Then where he at? I came to you because you in charge of the shit, and if he did fuck it up, it's still your fault." I squatted in front of him.

"Look, I ain't never shorted, you have I? I never misplaced shit in years, Jay. I been loyal," he said, deciding to stand up and face me.

"Jay." Duane pulled me aside.

"The lil homie got a point, bruh." He came closer to me so nobody would hear us rapping.

"I know, but how can you cut off the arm without also cutting off the hand?" I asked.

He looked confused as hell, which I expected.

"I can come out here and run shit for you, Jay. The nigga ain't did shit. Let's find the nigga we need to find, and I can set up shop out here for a little bit."

I was still pissed about his bullshit when it came to Aaron dying, but he was my brother, and we never fell out too long.

"I like the idea of having a nigga I trust out here overseeing shit. Okay, bet. If this nigga even piss sideways though, lil bro…" I pointed the shears at Lil Nick.

"I hear you," Duane said and stepped off.

I watched him walk Lil Nick out.

"You stay here too, Q."

I looked at one of my goons and nodded.

I loved my brother, but I had a bad feeling that couldn't be shaken for some reason. Something was off about this shit.

Duane

My plan was finally coming together. I was gonna start in San Francisco and work my way back to LA. I was fit to do more, and Jay was treating me like some low-level ass nigga. It's cool, he was gonna fuck up, and I would be right here to watch. To be real, I love my brother, but he always had the better of everything. When we were younger, my mother would always show him special attention because her thot ass got pregnant by a white dude, so she though Jay was special. I always resented that shit.

"Duane, what the fuck takin' so long?" Yvonne asked.

I rolled my eyes and kept rolling the weed.

"Shut the fuck up before you don't smoke," I told her.

I invited her to San Francisco for the weekend, and now she was getting on my nerves. She got quiet and watched TV. I handed her the jay and noticed that my phone was ringing. It was Tiffany. See, I had set me and Tiffany up in a nice ass spot right on the bay. And I got a lil apartment for Yvonne when she came through on the next block.

"That's the bitch, huh? I wish you'd leave her already," Yvonne said and pulled the lighter off the table.

"For what? Baby my wife, and you my hoe. Even if I left her, I ain't sure I'ma be fuckin' with you, so…" I shrugged and hit the reject button on Tiffany.

I hadn't been in the house since Friday, and it was now Sunday evening.

"Well, fuck it all, then. I can get me a fit nigga with some money," she said and pulled on the weed I just rolled.

I smirked and nodded.

"Come here, bae. That was wrong."

I got up and acted like I was about to cup her face. She smiled, and when I got closer, I closed fist punched her right in the nose.

"Arrrgghhh," she cried and fell on the floor.

"I'm boutta go home to my wife. Go the fuck back to LA, and if I hear about you entertaining other niggas, my fat ass gonna lay across your face and suffocate your stank ass."

I grabbed my duffle and threw some money on the bed and some weed.

"I won't be back," she said, obviously not understanding.

I walked over to where she sat on the floor and kicked her in the face. She was out cold. When she woke up, she would have a better understanding.

I left and got in my car to drive the block to my house. When I got there, Tiffany was putting luggage into the car.

I got out and went to grab the bags.

"I'm leaving. I know you was holed up with some bitch all weekend. I can do better than you, Duane.

"Really? You really think I need other bitches? Look at you, bae. I was on a run getting us this." I opened the bag and showed her the stacks of money.

Her eyes lit up just like I knew they would.

"Well, why didn't you answer the phone?" she whined.

"Did you not see my charger by the bed? You know my shit

fucked up and I gotta use the charge pad," I lied.

I started telling her that so she would think my phone was always dead.

"Well, we gonna go get you a new one" She pulled out a stack and kissed my cheek.

"That's my baby." I smacked that fat ass and took her bags inside.

My phone vibrated in my pocket. Tiffany was upstairs putting her shit back, so I answered.

"Aye, what's good, Sammi?"

"Bruh, its niggas asking the right questions for Jay, man. It's gonna come back to us," he said.

"The number you have dialed is not in service." Then I hung up.

What the fuck? This nigga rapping over the phone. Yeah, I got Aaron's ass. He didn't want to get down, so he laid down. Sammi had agreed because he was greedy as fuck. I knew how good Jay paid him as a goon, but he still wanted more. I was gonna kill his ass when I took the throne.

"Baby, who is Yvonne?" I heard Tiffany ask.

"Huh." I turned around like I didn't hear her.

"You heard me, you fat fucker!" She held a piece of paper, and I snatched it out her hand.

This bitch.

She wrote me a love letter and intentionally put that shit in my bag.

"Aight, fuck it, man. She's my girl, and before you start the theatrics, I ain't gonna stop fuckin' her, and you ain't leavin'. Go finish putting the shit up," I said and walked into the kitchen.

I could hear her crying, and it hurt me to hear it, but at least I was being honest. I needed a bitch with thick skin like Kola to help me run the new empire I was building. Tiffany had to fall in line.

Kola

Me and my friends landed in South Beach on Jay's private jet a little after the sun went down. We had been cordial, but not back like we should have been by now. I loved him, but I didn't want him to feel like he owned me. He already knew I wasn't with the shit.

I texted him to let him know that I landed, and he texted me back that he knew that, and he loved me. I smiled as we walked out to the front of the airport to get to the rentals.

"Mrs. Wells?" a big Spanish dude walked up and said.

I didn't know who this nigga was and why he was calling me by Jayson's last name.

"Who the fuck are you?" I asked, all set to dig in my bag for my gun.

"Phone call for you." He said and handed me a phone.

"Hello," I yelled after snatching the phone from him.

"Babe, stop being difficult for no reason. Get in the fuckin' car," Jay said then hung up.

Shay and Diamond didn't know what to do. I waved them to come on, and we got in the limo. There was a bottle and a note next to it.

Bae, I love you, and I'm sorry.

I smiled and picked up the bottle of Grey Goose and the weed.

"Your nigga like that, bitch!" Diamond yelled.

We rolled and smoked the whole way to wherever this nigga was driving us.

We turned up until we pulled in front of a yellow and white mansion. The driver came out and opened the door for us.

"Bitch, who house is this?" Shay asked.

"I don't know," I responded.

I called Jay, but he didn't answer. What the hell was he up to?

"Here you go," the guy said and passed me keys. "The cars are in the garage, and the boat keys are here too," he said.

I jumped up and down and called Jayson again.

"Don't try to be all up on me now." He laughed when he answered the phone.

"Thank you so much, baby. I didn't even see inside the house yet." I squealed.

"Well, enjoy yourself, baby. I love you."

"I love you too," I gushed and hung up.

We ran into the house, and we all screamed.

"We shitting on everybody this weekend, bitches," I said as I looked around the all white living room.

The fireplace was lit, and I could smell food cooking. We walked into the huge kitchen and there was a woman dressed as a chef.

"Hi, I'm Mila, your personal chef. I'm preparing tacos, lime chili shrimp, and mixed vegetables with rice."

It smelled good in this mufucka too. I couldn't wait to get home so I could show my nigga how much I appreciate this shit.

I toured the rest of the house, and when I saw the backyard, I damn near felt like a kid. It looked like a water park; this shit was off the hook. I went to the garage to see what was in there, and when I opened the door, I screamed for Shay and Diamond to come look. It was a pink Nissan GT-R and a purple Audi R8.

"We boutta be some stuntin' ass bitches," Diamond said, running in the garage and checking the cars out. After we ran around for a while, I went into the biggest bedroom and fell back onto the double king bed.

I didn't know what we would do after we ate, but I know I was taking one of the cars so we could flex out there.

***

We were four days into our vacation when I realized I hadn't talked to Jay since we got there. I decided to call him while I was in the tub. He liked talking nasty, and I was in the right position to be nasty with him.

The phone rang and rang, but he didn't pick up. I started to get alarmed because he always checked on me. I called Blaze, and he answered right away.

"Wassup, Kola?" he said.

"Where's Jay?" I asked, cutting past the pleasantries.

"I haven't seen him since the other night. He got pissed about something at y'all place, and he kicked me out."

What the fuck happened that made him mad, and why didn't he call and tell me?

"Aight, thanks."

I hung up and called Jay again, and this time the phone picked up.

"Hello." A female voice came through the phone.

I must have dialed the wrong number. I looked at my phone and saw that I hadn't.

"Who the fuck is this?" I screamed on the bitch.

"Who the fuck is this? Bitch, you the one who called!" she retorted.

Oh, I was heading home.

"Who the fuck you on my phone with?" I heard Jay yell.

I felt like I got punched in the gut. I could hear them tussling and a slap.

"Kola," he said breathlessly.

"Who the fuck is that, Jay?" I asked.

I could feel my body trembling with anger. I heard yelling from the female then the phone hung up. I threw my phone in the water and got out the tub, nice and calmly. I dried off, got dressed, and packed my bags. I was about to fuck California up.

Jay

Fuck! I don't know why I let this bitch talk me into coming over there. I knew Kola was on her way home, and shit was about to hit the fan. I had been doing good at dodging Ashley's advances, and my anger had me fail this time. Shit, all Ashley was to me was some pussy, and I should have never fucked her ass when I came and vented to her. what the fuck was I thinking.

Shit, I was already feeling some type of way because Kola didn't want to give a nigga baby. I got stressed and said fuck her since she basically said fuck me. When I saw that paper from the doctor saying she was on birth control, I lost it. She had lied to me and over and over. Had me looking like a fool, thinking I'm trying for a baby when she blocked the shit anyway. Fuck it, the damage was done now, and I just had to deal with the consequences.

"What the hell does she have that I don't, Jay?" Ashley cried.

We had been tussling and shit, and I was tired and pissed.

"She has my heart, but you might have fucked that up!" I yelled.

"No, nigga, you fucked that up! I ain't the one who cheated, you did. But that bitch will never be me, and when you realize that, I'll be waiting."

"Man, whatever. Don't call my phone." I grabbed my phone and keys, and headed out the door. I needed to figure out how to get out of this shit without Kola killing my ass,

When I pulled up at the house, I sat in the car for a minute.

Shit was crazy, and I didn't know what the future held for me and Kola, but I knew I loved her ass. I tried to call Kola, but her phone kept going to voicemail. I wasn't feeling that shit, but what could I do? I just headed inside to wait for her because I knew her ass was on the way home. I had stopped at a few spots to kill time, but I ain't have shit to do but go home and wait to face whatever I had coming.

***

It had been a good eight hours since I had talked to Kola, and I was going crazy. Her girls weren't even answering the phone, and they were no longer at the mansion. I heard a car pull up, and I looked out the window. Sure enough, it was her ass. I prepared myself for the drama that was about to ensue. I had already smoked two blunts and was high as hell.

When Kola walked in the door, she looked at me, and I could tell that she was pissed.

"Where is your phone, and why the fuck is it going to voicemail?" I asked, trying to deflect from the real situation.

"Really, nigga? You had a bitch answering your phone and checking me, and the first thing you say to me is where's my phone? You got me all the way fucked up!"

Before I could respond, this crazy muthafucka pulled out a gun.

"Man, chill out. It ain't even what you think."

She smiled, and that shit scared me.

"You damn near forced your way into my life, made me love you, and then you cheat!"

Pow!

"Ah, fuck! Bitch, are you crazy?" She had shot me in the fucking foot.

"Call me another bitch!"

Yeah, her ass was fucking crazy.

"You just fuckin' shot me!"

"I know." She laughed.

Who the fuck was this chick? Because this was not my Kola.

"Look, let's talk about this. I didn't cheat on you. I mean, I was with her, but that's because I just needed to vent. I mean, you keep hollering about getting married and shit, but you won't even give a nigga a baby. You on birth control and shit, and I didn't even have an input in that shit. Yeah, I found your prescription! That's what made me mad enough to go fuck another bitch. I ain't saying I'm right, but I was fucked up in my head, baby. I swear that bitch ain't got shit on you, baby. That shit was wrong what you did, though."

"I love how you're trying to turn this shit around on me, but it's cool! I'm done with your trifling ass. You want that hoe you was with, well you are free to have her. Stay the fuck away from me, with your dirty dick ass!" She walked out the door, and I let her because I didn't need her crazy ass shooting me again, but please believe we were not over.

Kola had the game twisted if she thought I was letting her go for long.

*****

I hadn't seen Kola's ass in over two months, and I had no clue where the fuck she was. I had been looking high and low for her ass, but she was hiding good. She had even changed her phone number, and I was going crazy not being able to find my baby. Not to mention Ashley was driving me fucking crazy. She wouldn't stop calling me or popping up wherever I was, and I couldn't deal with that shit. I missed my girl, and I needed her like my fucking air. Shit was just all the way fucked up.

Kola

I couldn't bring myself to even reach out to Jay if I wanted to. He broke me, and fucked me good while doing it. I couldn't believe he cheated on me. I still couldn't wrap my mind around the shit. I got a whole new phone and service. Since I didn't have a home of my own anymore because I moved in with that bitch ass nigga, I was in a damn hotel. I didn't have anybody to turn to, and that hurt even more. I couldn't go to my friends and shit because they had they own shit going on, I only had me, which I always knew from the day the doctor slapped my ass.

I looked out the window of Chicken Confidential restaurant on Sunset. I got sick looking at the couples acting all happy and shit. *He ain't gonna do shit but cheat,* I thought as I saw the women smiling all happy and shit.

"Number 53," the loud ass Hispanic chick yelled out.

"Aye, throw some hot sauce packets in there," I told her.

She nodded and threw some in. When I was leaving, I bumped into Sammi, Jay's minion.

"Kola, where you been, man? You know Jay been looking for you and shit," he said all loud and shit.

"Tell Jay to go straight to hell, and you can join him. Y'all niggas knew he was cheating and shit, that's why I hate niggas. Y'all let bitches get played for a fool, and still call a bitch sis. Fuck outta here." I took my shit and left. I knew he was gonna call Jay, but I would be long gone.

"Aye, Kola!" I heard Sammi call out.

"What, nigga?" I said as he approached.

"Bae," Jay called out from Sammi's speaker.

I walked away, but Sammi followed.

"Man, come on, Kola. Where you staying?" He sounded desperate.

I still didn't say shit until I got to my car.

"Jay, you chose who you wanted. You can't come back to me. We over." I got in the car, but Sammi stopped me from leaving.

"Move!" I yelled at him after rolling my window down.

"He ain't moving, I'm on the way," Jay said.

"I will fucking run you over."

I put the car in drive and moved up. He still didn't budge. I saw that I could run over the curb and go across the grass to the street, and I did just that. His stupid ass tried to chase the car like he would actually catch me. I came down off the curb and got the fuck outta there. Fuck Jay.

*****

I couldn't imagine spending another night stuck in this hotel, so I was stepping out with Shay and Diamond to some hookah club they had come across. I admired my cat suit in the mirror, then threw on some gold hoops to set off the black. I grabbed my platform boots and adjusted my dreads, which I had in a bun. I was a banger for sure.

I looked around the hotel suite and felt so lonely for a minute, but after a shot, I was okay again.

The hotel doorbell outside the suite sounded. I went and opened the door since I knew it was Diamond. She was picking me up, and then we would go and get Shay. When I let her in, she had the same damn catsuit I had on, except the belly was cut out of mine.

"Biiiiiitch. Was you creeping through my closet?" I smacked my teeth.

"No, but of course we got the same taste." She set her Louis Viton bag down, and I admired it for a minute.

"He must have fucked up again," I said, almost certain it was new and from her cheating ass nigga. Like I said, we all have the same issues.

"Girl, he gave me this after I caught him having that Facebook video sex with a bitch. I'm telling you, I'm looking for place, and I'm leaving that nigga," she said for the 900th time.

She ain't never going nowhere.

"Well, fuck these niggas tonight." I started dutty winding.

"Yes, fuckem." She bumped asses with me.

"So, look, let's smoke and pour some to go cups." I went and got the to-go cups I got from Wal-Mart the other day. They had tops and straws.

"That's cool. I got some white widow." She did a happy dance.

"So, you ain't never tell me what happened with Jay," she said, breaking our fuck niggas rule for tonight.

"Girl, tried to make that clown nigga keep me where I was so he can come say sorry like he been saying. I still can't believe him, Diamond." I shook my head.

"All niggas do it, that's why ain't no point in looking for another because he gonna do it too. I gave up on faithful niggas a while ago. We some fine ass bitches, so if we can't stop 'em from straying, shit, who can?"

"I hear you, but I just can't grasp that concept. I mean, live how you want, but me, I need me a faithful one." I checked my nails after lighting the blunt because I thought I felt it chip.

"Respect. So, you know we need to speed this shit up because your friend gonna be blowing our phones up soon.

"I'm already hip. Let's finish this and go."

We kept talking shit then and finally left to get Shay. When we pulled up, she was cursing at her nigga from the front door.

"Yeah, fuck you too, punk mufucka," she said and slammed the door.

No breaks given for our clique. Now with her nigga, cheating wasn't the problem. He couldn't keep his damn hands to himself. They fought like Tyson and Holyfield all the damn time, and she got her fair share of wins from his punk ass. I told her to let me smoke his ass, but she won't let me.

"Hey hoes." She jumped in.

"Girl, fuckem!" I yelled as we drove off to have fun.

The line was stupid long, and I wasn't waiting at all, not even in the cut line. I walked to the door and dropped my name, and they let us in. I had my own pull, but with Jay, it knocked up all the way up. Ugh, why the hell did I have to incorporate everything with his ass.

"Let's get some drinks," I yelled over the music.

We stepped to the bar, and like magic, niggas flocked. One in particular gave me a tingle, so I let him rap to me.

"So, what's a baddie like you doing in a club and shit? You need to be home with a husband somewhere." He flashed his pearly white teeth.

He was cute as hell, and he looked like money.

"Nah, I guess I wasn't marriage material." I stirred my drink with my finger.

"I know we trying to be serious and all, but you are wearing that suit, girl. I love a thick ass bae. You gotta be like a 16 or 18 down there." He stepped back to admire my ass without shame.

"I'm a 16." I giggled.

"Good God, ma." He bit his lip and got closer to me.

"I swear, I would eat that pussy like you never had it ate. Thicker always taste better." He pulled my ear lobe into his mouth then moaned into my ear.

"I knew you taste like candy. I bet you even sweeter down there." He went back to my ear, but was stopped short by the cocking of a gun.

"You got three seconds to get away from my bitch, nigga." Jay had the gun pressed to the guys ear.

"Oh shit, homie. I ain't know she was here with somebody." The guy looked like he was about to pass out.

"Stop it!" I pulled the gun down.

The dude ran out as Jay turned to me.

"So, you letting that nigga whisper all in your ear and shit?" Jay asked as he tucked his gun.

I noticed he was dressed the fuck down.

"So, what you doing here?" I asked, gritting on him.

"A few of my old friends got a party going on in VIP." He waved to the bartender.

"That's good."

I got up and walked past his dumb ass. I knew my friends were right behind me from the heels clacking. I don't know why I wanted to cry from just being right there with him.

"Move," Jay said and pushed my friends aside.

"You really think this shit a game, huh? You don't get to leave me, baby. I already love you, and that shit means too much to me to lose it." Jay pulled me into a small, empty corner by the bathroom.

"Why you playin' this stupid ass game, man?" he said, turning red.

"See, you don't get it. It's not a game. You think I'm supposed to just sit by and let you make a fool of me? Fuck no. I was good on my own, and I'm still good man. You need to be better to the next bitch and save all this shit for whoever she is. You did me wrong as fuck for no reason, Jayson. Matter of fact, go be with the bitch you just had to break my heart for. What's wrong? She wasn't worth it, huh? Yeah, I know." I wanted to steal his ass.

"You right, bae. I wasn't shit for that, but I swear it was just a dumb ass moment. I been walking around with something just in case I ran into you." He pulled out a box and opened it. It was a beautiful ring, and he grabbed my hand. "I want to marry you, Kola."

I looked at the ring then at him. I couldn't do it.

"No, I don't want to marry you anymore. I wanted to marry the Jayson who would do anything to have me and keep me. Not a nigga who pull a ring just to say I'm sorry. You don't get it, Jay. You so used to taking what you want that you don't give others what they need."

I closed the box and walked past him. No sooner than I got an inch away, I let the tears flow. I loved him so much, I just couldn't be stupid for him.

Jay

Fuck! I was lost. I had fucked up and didn't know how to fix this shit. A nigga had been going crazy as fuck without Kola. I felt like a straight up bitch. I couldn't eat, barely slept, and I barely came out the fucking house. I needed my bitch back, and I wasn't stopping until I got her. I had been in a few relationships, but ain't shit compared to this one. That was my fucking heart, and I needed her to get that shit. Yeah, I fucked up, but I was only human.

I watched her walk out the club alone, and I followed her. I could tell she was upset because she wasn't paying attention to where she was going and bumped into the same guy that I pulled a gun on. What pissed me off was this nigga had the nerve to still be cheesing in her face.

I walked right up them and popped his ass right in the fucking head. Good thing no one was out here, I had a silencer, and we weren't near a camera.

"Really, nigga?" she yelled, and I grabbed her ass up.

"Shut the fuck up before you draw attention to us. I just told that nigga to get out yo face, yet here he is again."

"Nigga, you don't get to stake claim on me! We are not together!"

"Nah, we together forever, ma. You took a break, but that shit is over. We about to go home and work this shit out." I dragged her ass straight to my car and threw her in there before hitting the locks. I got in and pulled off.

"You fucking crazy. How you kidnapping me though, Jay? My friends don't even know I'm gone."

"Well, call they asses and tell them. Shit, I don't give a fuck. We about to hash this shit out and stop running from our problems."

Yeah, I was a crazy ass nigga, but I didn't give a fuck. Kola made me go there.

It was hell getting her in the house because she fought me, but here we were. I had been trying to talk to her for the past hour, but her ass was straight ignoring me.

"I got all the time in the world, so whenever you ready talk, ma."

"Fuck you!"

"You so fucking sexy when you're mad, baby."

She rolled her eyes.

I sat there and watched her for a minute before walking over to her. she was sitting on the bed with her legs crossed. The body suit she had on had my dick hard as fuck.

"Get the fuck away from me!"

I pushed her ass back on the bed and climbed on top of her.

"No, Jay, move!" she whined, but she wasn't mean about it. That let me know she was horny, and daddy was about to fix it for her.

I unzipped her, catsuit, releasing her breasts.

"Really, nigga? You think this is gon' fix shit? Well it's not, so move." She tried to push me away, but I was stronger.

I grabbed one of her breasts and took the nipple in my mouth. She tried not to moan, but she failed.

"Jay, move please! I don't want you no more."

She was crying, and I felt like shit. I hated that she was hurting, but I just wanted to make her feel good. I leaned up and pulled her clothes off. She let me, but she was laying there looking off into space. That shit fucked with me.

I slid her thong off and dove head first into the pussy. She was crying, but I knew it was feeling good because she was wet as fuck. I mean, the pussy was juicy.

Not too long after, she was cumming in my mouth. I sucked it all up then climbed back on top of her. I unzipped my pants and pulled my dick out.

"Can I feel you?"

She didn't respond. I turned her face so that she was looking at me.

"I love you, bae, and I'm sorry."

She still didn't say shit.

I slid into her, and she wrapped her legs around me. I moved in and out of her slowly, hitting her g-spot every time. She was crying, and I kissed every fucking tear away. I swear, if she ever forgave me, I would never hurt her again. It fucked with me heavily that she was hurting because of me.

"I love you so fucking much, Kola!"

She started fucking me back, and that shit was feeling so good.

"I want to get on top." She finally opened her mouth.

I pulled out and laid on my back. She mounted me and went to work. Her pussy was so fucking good and fit me perfectly. She was riding the shit out of me, but for some reason, this felt like the last time. I said a silent prayer to God. I needed him to help me make this shit right because I knew at this point he was the only one who could help me.

Kola had fucked me so good, a nigga fell asleep afterward. But, now I was woke, and she was gone. Fuck! My baby was gone, and it wasn't shit I could do about it, I knew she was gone for good too. That's what hurt the most.

I gotta move on, you aint no good for me........
Kola

I loved Jay with everything in me, but I was hurt, and I didn't forgive easily. He was the one person I never thought would hurt me, and it was no coming back from that.

"Sis, you heard me?" Shay said, clapping her damn hands in my face like she was crazy.

"Yeah, I heard you. I think you should take the shit back and give him the ring," I said, looking at the wedding dress she had picked out.

"Okay, look. I get that you going through something, but you don't get to shit on everybody else's happiness," Shay said, looking at me then Diamond.

"Happiness? What happiness, Shay? He treats you like a best friend with benefits, and when he ain't doing that, he beating your ass. I cut my losses, and you need to do the same."

I stormed out of David's Bridal, only to be caught by Diamond.

"You wrong as shit for that, you know," she said with a scowl.

"How, I'm just telling the truth, and you know it." I snapped my neck.

"Regardless, you're her friend, just like I am. We all got our shit, and how the fuck dare you judge her?" She snapped her neck right back.

"Look, the fact that she is my friend makes me look out for her. I don't want her to get hurt, Diamond. You see that big ass bruise on her shoulder? Or are we just gonna ignore the shit? You know what? I have to go check this apartment out. Tell her I'm sorry, and I didn't mean it."

"No, you tell me. Tell me how my best friend so jealous, she can't be there for her friend," Shay said.

"Jealous of what, bitch? I was tryin' to help your dumb ass, but be like me and stay stupid until it blows up in your face. Let's all just leave and start over." I broke down crying, and they both came to comfort me.

"I'm sorry!" I screamed.

"It's okay," Shay said, rubbing my locs.

"Why the fuck he do that shit to me, Shay?"

I felt sick about how Jayson had betrayed me. He was so wrong for this shit.

"He stupid. He didn't know what he had, sis," Diamond said and sniffled. She was crying too.

"Come on, I'm gonna reschedule. We can get some tacos, smoke, and watch movies the rest of the day." Shay squeezed my hand.

"You know what, no. I'm too strong for this bullshit. Let's do what we came here to do. I'm sorry about that shit." I straightened up. "Nah, matter of fact, we can go to Vera Wang and get you the best dress we can find and run up a bill. I can at least hit his ass in his pockets."

I went into my wallet and pulled out Jay's American Express

that he always let me hold. It wouldn't heal my heart, but it would damn sure feel good.

On our way down Rodeo, I spotted a restaurant for sale and decided to take the number down. Without Jay, I couldn't move weight, but I loved to cook. I could take classes to refine and shit, but yeah, I could do this. I didn't need Jay, and I was gonna prove it to him.

****

Several months later

I sat across the table from Derrick at Cheesecake Factory as he tried to apologize about what happened on the phone two years ago. He had hit me on Instagram and asked me to lunch. I said fuck it. I wasn't doing shit but worrying myself over me and Jayson, and I needed some fresh air from the hotel. Ugh, which reminded me that I was supposed to look for a new place.

He was still sexy as hell too. I saw all that sexy from the car when he was waiting for me to walk up.

"Kola, you not even listening to me," he said and leaned back in his chair.

"I'm sorry, my mind is kind of fucked up. I'm all over the place right now." I watched the waiter come over, so I grabbed the menu.

"Well, what happened with you and your nigga? That's the dude you curved me for, right?" He chuckled.

"I ain't curve you. You wasn't available. But really, I don't wanna talk about that. How you been?" I asked and sipped my long island down.

"Well, I wanna talk about it. Tell me what not to do, so I don't fuck up..." he said, trying to run game.

"Are you guys ready to order?" The waiter came back after giving us a few minutes.

"Yes, were gonna have some fried cheese, buffalo wings with blue cheese, fried ravioli too. You can get the entrée when you come back," Derrick told her.

"You goin' to the electric chair, fool?" I asked, thinking of all the appetizers he had just ordered.

"We got a lot to talk about." He smirked.

We ate the appetizers, but I declined to get an entrée. Talking to him was cool, and it kind of distracted me.

Derrick was walking me to my car when I saw Duane's fat ass walking toward us with his hoe ass girlfriend. I never liked how that bitch looked at Jayson.

"What's up, Kola? When you left Jay, you left us all." He smiled.

"Hey, Duane." I rolled my eyes because he probably knew Jay was cheating too.

"Hey, Kola. Girl, who your friend?" Tiffany asked with her head cocked to the side.

"Hey," I said dryly, but not answering her question about Derrick.

"You need to call my brother instead of running around with the next nigga," Daune said and mugged me.

"Nigga, fuck you. He put his dick where he shouldn't, and shit is done. Just because this gutta hoe let you fuck Twinkies and other bitches don't mean I'ma let my nigga run around." I barked at him, ready to pull my gun.

"Oop, bitch please. My nigga stays faithful because I make sure he ain't gotta do that shit." She mugged me.

"Baby, please shut up. He was at Jay's fight party with some Mexican bitch. They went and fucked in the bathroom. Had the bitch smellin' like bacon grease." I cackled.

"Don't make me whoop our ass out here, bitch," Duane said and stepped to me.

"My nigga, step to a man. Fuck you mean," Derrick said and got between us.

"Did I acknowledge this nigga?" Duane pointed at Derrick.

"You ain't have to, cuh. Shawty say she ain't fuckin' with ole boy, and I don't give a fuck if you tell him." Derrick pulled me with him and walked to the car.

"Fuck him. Thanks for lunch, Derrick. Get them crazy hoes in line." I smiled and jumped into my car.

"Let me get your number. We ain't gotta talk on Instagram only." He flashed his sexy ass smile.

I ran him my number but made it clear I wasn't trying to jump into anything. Of course, he lied and said that he agreed, but I can tell by the look he gave that he was trying to give me the full court press.

I looked at the time and saw that I could make it to see this lil two-bedroom house in Rancho Cucamonga. I didn't even wanna do shit too flashy because I had just bought a hair salon instead of the restaurant. It was in in Beverly Hills as well, and I knew I could probably make good money out there. I was proud of myself. I know I flip birds best, but until I can get back on, this was what I had to do.

After checking out the house, I decided to take it. I had some shit in storage from my house in the hills, so I was happy. I already had furniture at least. Since Derrick wanted to get on my good side, I would use that to my advantage and get him to help me move the shit. I felt like this was another step away from Jay, getting my own place again.

Jay

I threw myself into work amongst other shit. It was hard not seeing Kola. This time, she really had left, her friends didn't even know where she was. A nigga was hurt, but I was managing. It wasn't shit I could do to make her take me back. Kola wasn't some weak bitch, and I respected that. Doesn't mean I had to like it, though.

I had met this cute little chick, but she was only good for busting a nut. I wasn't looking for a relationship. That shit was on hold for Kola if and when she ever came back.

Shit, it's been four months, and I ain't heard a word from her. Every so often I go to her social media to see if she posted, and all she ever posts is shit like, life is good. That's my only indication that she's still breathing.

"Aye, man, you seen this shit?"

Sammi walked in the media room where I was watching the game. He passed me his phone, and it was a picture of Kola with a dude moving stuff into a house. They were smiling and shit. I was really hurt now because she had moved on. I still had one of my niggas checking for her.

"What the fuck you showing me this shit for? Fuck her!"

Sammi looked at me funny, but I didn't give a fuck. If Kola called herself trying to hurt me, that shit worked. I got up and walked out the room because a nigga was truly in his feelings. I called Trina, the chick I had been smashing. I needed a fucking release.

"Hey, Jay," she answered.

"Get naked, I'm on my way."

"Yes, daddy."

From this point on, it was fuck it. I was done trying.

After fucking with Trina, I had some shit to do for my mother. A few minutes after I got there, she was already talking shit about me and Kola.

"Well, who you got to blame but yourself?" my mother asked as she flipped through channels on her TV. She insisted on bringing Kola up every time I saw her, and it was annoying as fuck.

"Damn, you ain't got nothin' else to talk about?" I asked her.

"Yeah, your father came again, wanting to build something with you." She coughed into a napkin.

"I don't care shit about him. Look how he did us. Stop talkin' to him," I said and moved the table with her food on it to the side

"He sick, boy. He just wanna talk to you," she said and looked up at me.

"Good, he gonna want that shit for a while. Did you need anything else? I went and got you everything you need from Walmart. All the food put up too," I told her.

"Thank you, I don't know where I would be without you, Jayson." She got up and hugged me.

"No problem. I love you, ma." I kissed her cheek.

"I think she still loves you. You were wrong, son. I promise, all you have to do is win her back and mean it. What the fuck possessed you to cheat on her?" she asked, starting the very conversation I had tried to avoid.

"She was on birth control while I was trying to start a family, all because I ain't try to marry her right away," I said, finally letting her know why I was angry and fucked up.

"Bullshit, so you wanna get her pregnant but not commit? Sounds like you need to be angry at yourself," she said and sat back on the bed.

"Yeah, aight, man. I gotta bounce." I walked out of my mom's spot in Imperial Garden and jumped in my car. She didn't wanna move, and I was tired of trying to make her.

After I left my mother's, I decided to stop at the liquor store and grab a soda and a pack of Black and Milds. My phone lit up, and it was Ashley, still trying to get me to call her ass. She was dumb as fuck if she thought I was going to deal with her in any type of way. I decided to play around with her ass.

"What, man?" I answered.

"Jay, I been trying to call you," she said and sniffled into the phone.

"Duh, what the fuck you want?" I asked.

"I'm pregnant, Jay. I'm almost five months, and I'm just finding out," she cried.

"Well, what the fuck you telling me for? You better find your baby father. The fuck." I said and hung up on her.

She must have taken me for a clown ass nigga or something. I knew she wasn't pregnant by me. I always strapped up, and I don't remember no condom breaking.

My phone vibrated, and she had sent me a text.

Ashley: *Well we gon have to just go to court when its born.*

I blocked her ass from texting my phone. I ain't have time for her bullshit. She was trying to trap a nigga like I was dumb or something.

I sped off after leaving the store and decided to call Duane to see how money was looking. I still let him handle a lot of shit, but I was fully running my empire now.

"Yeah, where you at?" I asked him, already driving toward his house,

"I'm at home. I was just about to call you, though," he said, breathing heavier than usual.

"Nigga, what the fuck? You runnin'?" I asked, but seriously doubted that shit.

"Hell no. I'm fuckin', nigga." He grunted.

"Why the fuck would you answer the phone?" I hung up and headed to his house anyway.

We had a new gun distributor, and he had better weapons at cheaper prices than the nigga I was just dealing with.

I saw this thick legged chocolate chick walking and swore that was Kola until she turned around. I sighed like a bitch and kept driving. I was a damn fool to fuck up with Kola, and I knew it. Even after I said fuck her, I rode up the steep hill and pulled into the driveway. I banged on the door, and Tiffany came running out with a silk robe open. She was ass naked underneath.

"Tell his fat ass to come on," I told her, ignoring her usual shit that she does when I come around.

I walked in and sat down in the living room. I could smell the body wash, and noticed that her hair was wet. He must be in the shower because I didn't hear him yet.

"You know we saw Kola with some dude." She walked up to me after closing the door.

"So, what the fuck you tellin' me for?" I shrugged like it

didn't make me hot.

"I was just saying, damn. So, who you fucking with now? I know you already got a bitch." She sat on the couch, and her robe was fully opened. Her titties sat up perfectly, and her thighs looked delicious.

"Duane," I called upstairs.

"He passed out after he fucked me." Tiffany opened her legs to show me her pink, clean shaven pussy.

"You need to stop, man. I ain't fuckin' with you like that." I laughed at her ass.

I heard movement upstairs. Tiffany closed her robe and shot up the steps.

I shook my head at her scandalous ass. It was one thing to look, but I would never fuck my brother's bitch.

She came back down with a pair of shorts and a tank top on.

"He knocked the lamp over in his sleep. You might as well do what you gotta do without him. Pussy put niggas to sleep." She smirked and started to buss down a cigar.

"Man, what the fuck?" I shook my head in irritation because this nigga was just coming back from San Francisco, and he had been lazier than usual.

"I can try to wake him up," she offered, but I shook my head and left.

I followed the directions to a small cleaners in South Central LA. I ain't feel like the traffic, but I had to see what this nigga was talking about with these guns. I must have been crazy as fuck for coming to meet a nigga I didn't know. I stayed strapped, so I wasn't scared of niggas wanting to gun ball and shit.

I walked in and saw a small, Asian woman sitting on a stool

next to the register.

"I need to see D."

That was all I had to go off of. Duane's simple ass was supposed to be the liaison and shit, so all this shit was something he setup.

A lanky ass Spanish dude walked out the back and waved for me to come."

I followed him to a small office in the back where I faced a nigga I had never seen before, not even on the police radar when I was on.

"You must be Jay. I'm Derrick, D for short." He got up and shook my hand while motioning for me to sit down.

"Oh, okay, my brother tells me you giving up crates for the low." I leaned back in my chair and pulled out a cigar full of weed.

"We don't smoke in here, my nigga," D said.

"I do."

I blew smoke out and looked at him, wondering why the fuck he wasn't continuing the conversation. I didn't have all day.

His nigga looked like he was ready to jump, but I was ready for his big ass too.

"That's aight, open the window," he told the dude.

"So, who is your brother?" he asked, but for some reason, I had the feeling he knew already.

"Nigga, you don't know the niggas you call meetings with?" I said, getting agitated.

The door suddenly opened, and we all turned around to see who was walking in on us.

When I saw Kola, I didn't even have shit to say.

"Jay, what the hell are you doin' here? Derrick, what the fuck is this?" she asked the dude.

Then it made sense. Derrick was the nigga in her phone, the ex.

"Kola, come in, sexy. I been waiting for you," the nigga Derrick said. He set this shit up.

"So, you knew who I was already, you just wanted me to see you with my bitch? Damn, she must still be callin' a nigga name when y'all fuck to go this far." I got up, and Kola watched my every move.

"You really went this far? Fuck this, if you making this shit a game, I'm done." Kola stomped out the office, and I went behind her ass.

"So, that's you, huh?" I asked and grabbed her arm.

"I moved on. You been moved on, so why the fuck can't I?" she asked with a single tear coming down her cheek.

"This nigga set you up to see me so he could fuck with a nigga's head, and you think that nigga the one. He can't give you what the fuck I can, girl." I grabbed her up and kissed her.

"Stop, you ain't good for me, Jay. I knew that a whole two years ago, and you proved it to me. You didn't cheat because you was mad, you cheated because you wanted to, nigga. I'm sorry about this shit and what he did, and I will have words with him," she said as she walked to the front.

"You know we ain't over, man. Don't do this shit. This nigga a fuck boy, baby." I pulled her to me.

"Jay, we done. You made a choice, and now I'm making mine. You fucked us up, not me," she said and left out the front door.

I walked back to the office and clapped for the nigga.

"You don't want this beef, my nigga. Don't play these type of games with me, bruh. Because no matter what you think you and baby girl got, she gon' always want me." I pulled my gun out and shot his guard who stood next to him in the head.

"Consider that a warning shot," I said and left.

"Ain't no bitches over here, Jay, and tell your fat ass brother if he want it, he can still get it," he yelled.

This was the dumb shit I was talking about with my brother. He didn't even know who the fuck we were really meeting. I should have gone back in there and bloodied the whole spot up, but I didn't want niggas to know they got to me and shit.

Instead, I watched Kola back out the space she was parked in and get the fuck gone. All I could do was think about how beautiful she looked, even with hate filled eyes full of tears. It was something I just couldn't let go of. If she needed her lil time, cool. But she was gonna come home, and I didn't care what I had to do. I looked back at the cleaners I had just left and smirked. Bitch ass nigga.

***

I made sure to text Duane's ass and tell him what happened? He called me back, apologizing and shit, but it didn't even matter. He was about to be working at 7-11 fucking with me. I couldn't stop thinking about Kola and how she moved on to the next nigga that fast. A fuck nigga at that. I got pissed thinking about that pussy nigga touching my bitch, and I was ready to go shoot that cleaners up, but that nigga would know I was in my feelings, so fuck it.

I got home in time to see my maid leaving for the day. She was an older black woman named Sophia, and she loved Kola. I could tell she felt some type of way about what went down between us. She had barely said two words to me since Kola left.

She walked right past me and got into her car. She rolled her eyes at me, and I smiled and shook my head. My phone rang, and the number was blocked. I ignored it because I don't answer that type of shit. A text came though shortly after.

Unkown: *It's your father.*

Me: *Fuck you, I ain't got a father.*

Unknown: *Meet me.*

Me: *lol bruh, just move on, I don't want shit from you nigga. Where your wife? Bitch dead, huh? Now you wanna reach out.*

He didn't text back after that. I didn't give a fuck what he wanted, that nigga could suck a whole dick. I watched Martin and cleaned some of my guns. It was a force of habit since being with LAPD. I set the last gun down and leaned back on the couch, thinking of how lonely this shit was. I worked my ass off to get Kola, and I let her leave. Now, all I had was a string of hoes I didn't give a fuck about. I kicked the coffee table over and thought about how I had fucked up. I still felt like Kola was wrong as shit for being on birth control, but my response was downright fucked up. I heard two knocks on my door, causing alarm. I grabbed my .40 and walked to the door and looked through the peep hole.

What the fuck?

I opened the door and looked the fat, white dude up and down. He was holding a thin envelope pressed against his stomach.

"Yeah?" I barked.

"Jayson Wells. You've been served." He pushed the envelope into my hand and ran off.

I opened the envelope and read the request for paternal determination by Ashley's dumb ass. That bitch was delusional as fuck. I called Ashley, and she picked up on the first ring.

"Damn, they move fast," she said in a happy tone.

"Bitch, I ain't fucked you. You need to go find your baby father before mufuckas can't find you," I yelled.

"Well, I did. I'm getting an amnio DNA test so you can know before the baby is born. Oh, and the toilet was broke that day you went to flush your condom. I'm glad you tie them." She cackled.

"You nasty bitch!" I hung up and stomped on my phone. This bitch trapped the fuck outta me.

I went to put my shoes on because I was about to kill this bitch. What type of nasty ass shit was she on? I went to the door and stopped, laughing at myself. I put my gun down and went to sit on the couch. I did this shit to my fucking self.

You leave one situation to double the bullshit with another...   *Kola*

"Nigga, what the fuck kind of shit you on, cuh? Why the fuck would you do that shit? You don't know him, and he ain't gonna be cool," I said to Derrick as he sat on his couch and looked through his phone.

"Man, fuck that nigga. You know I ain't no bitch ass nigga," he said, pissing me off because he was in his phone and not paying attention to the conversation.

"It don't matter. You using me for your male pride bullshit. You got me fucked up. Don't call my phone," I said then got up and grabbed my purse.

"Man, come here. I'm sorry, aight? I just wanted the nigga to know you was straight now." He grabbed my hand.

"Straight, how? We ain't on no official shit. And doing shit like you did today ain't gonna make me want to." I rolled my eyes at his ass.

"You sure that's what it is? That nigga said something in the hallways that got you in your feelings."

"Nigga, he was my dude. We broke up, and you think I ain't feeling some type of way? Man whatever. I ain't boutta keep going back and forth with your ass." I opened the door, and he closed it.

"You ain't leaving," he said and slowly unbuttoned my shirt.

I pushed his hands off, and he grabbed my hands and put them over my head.

"I can love you betta than that nigga ever could." He kissed me and let his hands roam down my ass. I really wasn't in the fucking mood, so I pushed him off.

"You on punishment, nigga. Get your shit together."

I left out the door and could hear him cursing. I laughed and headed to my car. Jay did get me in my feelings. I hated his ass so much, I wanted to cut his sexy ass when I saw him. I didn't give a fuck how sorry he called himself. I had slowly started to take my emotions back, though. There was no way I was gonna keep crying every night over him. I was sure he wasn't doing the same.

I started to drive off when I realized I was supposed to meet up with Diamond's ass. She had made a move to finally leave her man, and she was supposed to move in with me until she found her own spot. I called her from my Bluetooth.

"Hey, I'm already here. Where you at?" she said in an upbeat tone.

"I'll be there in about ten minutes. Girl, Derrick set up a meeting with Jay just so he could see that I was with him," I said in a quick breath.

"That's some fuck nigga shit, sis. Why the fuck would he do that? Did Jay say something to you?" she asked.

"Of course. Don't matter, though. I already bowed out. Look, I'ma see you when I get there." I said and hung up.

I made it home quickly so I wouldn't have Diamond waiting too long. When I pulled up, she was on her phone yelling at somebody. From what I could hear, she must have been yelling at her ex. When she saw me, she hung up and jumped out her truck.

"His dumb ass think it's a game." She smiled weakly and opened the passenger side to grab a bag.

"Ughh, bitch, how many bags you got?" I said, causing her to laugh, but I saw tears coming down the side of her face.

"I don't know what I'm gonna do. I ain't got money or nothing. I just got this damn truck and the breath in my body," she said, breaking down further.

"You got me and Shay. You can stay as long as you want," I told her and grabbed the bag out her hand.

"Thanks, sis," she said with a smile and grabbed another bag.

We got her all set up in my pool house, and she decided to lay down and said she would see me tomorrow. I could tell she was taking it hard. I decided to cook her something to eat and chill the rest of the night. I had gotten a text from Derrick asking if he could come over, and I ignored them all. As I lay in my bed, I wondered what the hell I was gonna do about my love life. Jayson had fucked me over, and Derrick annoyed me with that bullshit he did. I couldn't win in this game for shit.

*****

I looked up and saw that it was 6:30 in the fuckin' morning, and a motherfucker was knocking on my door ready to get hurt. I ran down the stairs full of fury.

"Who the fuck!" I swung the door opened and screamed in excitement.

"Lil baby don't know a nigga no more, huh?" my cousin from Mississippi, Goose, walked in.

"Nigga, how the hell you find me? And what you doin' in LA?" I asked, pulling him in. He still looked like Slim Thug.

"I went and saw Uncle Tommy, and his crazy ass let me know what was up. Goose was my mother's nephew. His father was my mother's brother.

"So, guess what?" He pulled out a blunt and sat back like it wasn't early as fuck.

I was happy to see his ass, but damn.

"I'm movin' to Vegas, shawty. It's time to bring my talents to the west coast. You still making money out here?" he asked.

"A lot of shit happened. We need to wait 'til later when I'm ready to drink to let you know it all." I giggled.

"Shit, well we can get this money together, ma. You need something?" he asked and handed me the weed.

"Nah, I can still run these streets if I wanted. Like I said, long story. Now I'm going the fuck back to sleep. You welcome to kick it. My home girl in the pool house, so don't go in there." I got up and took his weed with me.

"She fuckin'?" he asked.

"Know what? Bye. Call me later so we can meet up."

I watched his ass walk past me, and I let him out. He did make me think, though. But knowing Jay, if he heard I made a move, he would be on me. I smoked and wasted the high by going right back to sleep. A few hours later, I heard more banging.

I went to the door, ready to snap again, when I saw it was Derrick's ass.

"I told you I would call your ass. Derrick, why you poppin' up at my shit like you crazy?" I said through the door.

"Kola, stop playin' before I break this mufucka down," he said through clenched teeth. I shook my head and opened the door.

"What?" I asked as I let him in. Damn, he smelled hella good.

"We really can't just move the fuck on? I ain't been shit but good to you since we linked back up." He grabbed for me and snatched me up by the waist.

"Move on to what, some fuckin'?" I smirked because I figured he was just trying to finesse himself some pussy.

"No, like the shit we had. You dumped a nigga for no reason, and then went and got a whole nigga. Here I am still trying to win your ass over, girl. I said I fucked up, I already know."

He pulled a large square box out and opened it. There was a rose gold locket with a chain that flowed with diamonds. He grabbed my arm and slid it on my wrist. It was ice cold.

"Damn, Derrick." I turned the bracelet over and opened the locket. It was a picture of him next to me while I was asleep. He was kissing me, and I was knocked out.

"I ain't trying to get my feelings hurt again, nigga. How I know you any different?" I seriously asked him.

"You don't, but what I ever do to you? We were together before, was you unhappy at all? Let me give you that shit again." He pressed me against the wall, held onto my waist, and looked me up and down as he licked his lips.

"Derr—"

He put his finger over my mouth and replaced the finger with his lips.

"Lemme love you the right way." He yanked my shorts down.

I stepped out of them and he lifted my leg up and dropped down to his knees.

"You always smell good," he said before parting my pussy lips like a whip with his tongue.

"Daaaamn." I grabbed the back of his head as he created waves in my pussy with his tongue. He was working the fuck out my clit right now.

"Your pussy taste like fruit, fuck." He stopped and planted kisses all over my kitty.

"Eat up, then, nigga." I pushed his head back into my pussy. I wanted a nice nut off this shit.

"Fuck, keep licking." I started to grind his face until I felt myself erupt. I almost drowned his ass.

He took his shirt off and wiped his face with it. I saw that his dick was hard, and I opened his belt for him and pulled his shorts down. I bit my lip as I thought about having it inside of me.

"Bend that thick ass over." He pushed his tongue into my mouth and turned me around.

He forcefully pushed himself into me, and I yelped at the first thrust.

"Mhhhm, take that dick." Derrick reached around and started playing with my clit.

My hard nipples slid up and down the cool wall while Derick sucked my neck, causing my pussy to respond. I started cumming again, I could feel it running down my legs.

"Fuck, you tryna make a nigga cum quick?" he asked, turning me around and quickly sucking on my nipples. He massaged my ass and bit down on my left nipple.

"Derrick, shit." I moaned, enjoying every bit of what he was doing.

"We going to bed." He pulled my arm, and I looked at him like he was crazy.

It was 9:00 in the morning. He still pulled me into the room then pushed me onto the bed.

"I'ma fuck you to sleep."

He came down, parted my legs, and went back to work. He wasn't playing when he said he was fucking me back to sleep. We didn't wake up until the next morning after three sessions of fucking. Even after that bomb ass sex, I was still as confused as ever. I wanted to believe he was keeping shit 100, but I didn't know what to trust anymore.

I let my guard down with Jay, changed how I carried myself, and even started dressing different, heels and shit. All for him to play me like a game of chess. Derrick could be on the same shit after a while like Jayson was, all in love until they not. I couldn't take another heartache, though. Fuck it, I was gonna take my time.

*****

10 months later

"Did you see how I did the rod, Kola?" Devon, one of the stylists in the salon asked me.

She had been trying to teach me how to do flexy rods and shit so I could get as much practice as possible. I wanted to start doing hair, and since I now had my cosmetology license, I was ready.

"Yeah, I saw," I said, looking at the text from Derrick and shaking my head.

"Then show me," she demanded.

"We can start again tomorrow," I said and started to walk out the door. Not waiting for her to say shit else.

I jumped straight in the car and headed home to see why it was urgent that he see me. I wanted to beat his ass because he forgot my damn birthday and didn't say shit to me before I left my house. I should have made his ass go home and block him. I pulled into the driveway and jumped out to kick his ass. When I got inside, I stopped dead in my petty ass tracks and covered my mouth.

There where so many balloons, it looked like a damn carnival. I walked down into the living room where there was a jewelry case smack dab in the middle of the l room. Derrick walked around the corner cheesing and holding a large box that he sat down at my feet. I could hear whimpers, so I tore it open, to be met by the cutest pit bull puppy. She had a diamond studded collar, and the name plate read *Princess*.

"Happy birthday." Derrick came in and pushed his tongue in my mouth.

"I thought you forgot, baby." I smiled and kissed him again.

I immediately tasted then smelled the liquor and got pissed off.

"I thought you weren't drinkin' no more, Derrick," I said and backed up, feeling disappointed that he lied to me yet again.

"I just had one man, damn," he slurred, clearly lying.

I guess I didn't realize how drunk he was when he walked up. We'd had a few incidents with him drinking, and I thought I was gonna have to kill his ass because he would get belligerent as fuck, and I wasn't no birdy that wouldn't go at his ass. He promised me that he wouldn't drink shit else because obviously when he did, he just fucked up. He waited until today to pull the shit.

"I swear." I stomped off into the kitchen and saw a bottle of Jack Daniels on the counter.

"Kola, come on, man. I got all this shit planned for us." He grabbed me around the waist.

"Well, go drink some water. I'm about to use the bathroom." I walked past him, still pissed.

He sobered up a little bit, and we went to Benihanas on Ventura. I couldn't wait to eat. I, of course, hit my friends in a text to let them know we was partying in a few hours. Derrick should be nice and sober by then, so he wouldn't show his ass.

Once we got inside, I looked around and waited as Derrick told the hostess it was us two. The food smelled so good that I was all in this chick's plate, trying to see what she was eating. Her baby was cute too. He was cooling in the car seat.

"Some nasty ass dude was in there lightin' the bathroom

up." I heard the voice that still even now sent a tingle up my spine. Jay pulled the chair out and sat down with the girl.

"Jay," I said, looking at the baby and seeing his face in the cute little boy.

"Kola." He stood up and dropped his eyes in shame. "Happy birthday, lil mama." He tried to hug me, but I stepped back.

"I see you got what you wanted, huh? This your baby mother?" I said, ready to cry at the sight of him with a family so fast.

"No, this ain't his mother," he said, not taking his eyes off me.

"Damn, Kola, you all in the nigga face," Derrick said, snapping me out my zone.

"Damn, you still fuckin' with this clown ass nigga? I know that nigga ain't handling you right." Jay said with a smirk.

"I handle all this chocolate you let go, bruh. You think she got anything on Kola?" Derrick said and pointed at the girl Jay was with, who now had a frown on her face.

"You might got me there." Jay winked at me.

"Jay, what the fuck?" the girl screamed, causing the baby to cry.

"Man, what the fuck you screaming for? You boutta be on the bus, man." Jay picked the tiny boy up and rocked him.

I felt jealous. For some reason, I felt regret.

"Kola, come on," Derrick snapped.

Jay turned to me and we locked eyes. I remembered why I hated him, but I also remembered why I loved him.

"Kola!" Derrick called for me again.

"I'm comin' damn," I yelled back and walked out behind him.

He zoomed in and out of traffic like he was crazy.

"Fuck that nigga, and you all in his face and shit," Derrick said out of nowhere.

"I wasn't in his damn face. You need to chill." I rolled my eyes.

"Don't make me snap on your ass, Kola."

He pulled over and jumped out. I didn't see where we were because I was busy telling Shay and Diamond what went down. I looked up and saw we were at one of his uncle's spots. The door opened to the place, and Derrick came out and jumped back in the car.

"What was that about?" I asked as he pulled off.

"Don't worry about," he said coldly and looked straight ahead.

I mugged his ass and let him keep driving. I didn't feel like going out, so I told him to just take me home, and I texted Shay and Diamond to tell them we could go out tomorrow.

Seeing Jay after all this time still hurt. Then he had a fucking baby too. I wished I would have just gone somewhere else, so I wouldn't have to see.

"Bae, I'm boutta step out." Derrick came in my room and leaned on the door, holding his phone and keys.

"Bye." I rolled my eyes and flipped the channels on my TV. "I guess you got somewhere to be on my birthday, but whatever. I might still go out." I cut my eyes at him.

"I was about to go get us some food so we can smoke and eat the rest of the night with your mean ass."

He turned his lip up and left. I kind of smiled because that was sweet of him, even though I was still pissed.

My phone lit up and I saw a text from a number that wasn't saved in my phone.

310-000-1234: Now my head gonna be fucked up for weeks, man. I still love you, Kola. Ain't shit changed. I don't even know if this the right number I'm texting. You still look like God blessed every bit of your ass too. I miss you, and I hope you text me back.

I locked my phone and shook my head, niggas will always say what you wanna hear. I opened the message and read it again then deleted it. Fool me once.

****

I was in a sound ass sleep when I was shaken awake.

"Kola, wake up," Diamond screamed.

"What the fuck, Diamond?" I jumped up, looking at her like she was crazy.

"Raj is here." She looked scared as hell.

"Man." I jumped up and grabbed my .22 out the nightstand.

When I saw the cable box read 2:38, I wanted to scream. I hate being woke out my sleep.

I ran down to the front door where this nigga was knocking at my fucking door like he was a fucking lunatic. I swung the door open, and he was standing there looking like a raging bull.

"Nigga, she left your stupid ass. Why the fuck you don't get it?" I asked, ready to drop his ass.

"This between me and my lady. What, you a trying to fuck her too? Fuck out my face." He waved me off.

I scratched my head with my gun.

"Raj, just leave. I told you not to come back here," Diamond said from the living room.

"He been here before?" I pointed the gun directly at him.

"Oh, she ain't tell you? We been fuckin' in the pool house since she moved in. I'm tired of these fuckin' games, Diamond. Get the fuck in here." He tried to come in, so I shot him in the arm.

He fell down holding it.

"What the fuck did you do, Kola?" Diamond came running from the living room to aid him.

"Shit. Crazy bitch!" He yelled at me.

"Baby, we gotta get you to a hospital," Diamond said, helping him up.

"You moved in here just to still do the same shit? Move your shit out, man." I slammed my door and locked it, then went to lock my back door.

What type of dumb shit was she on? All this shit was a waste of my fucking time. I went my ass back to bed after seeing them drive off.

I sat on my bed trying to doze off, and when I couldn't, I wanted to go hunt Raj and Diamond down to fuck them up.

I grabbed my phone and saw the texts I had missed when I was asleep. My cousin, Goose, had hit me, and so did Shay. I restored the text Jay sent me shortly after I deleted it. I didn't plan to hit him or anything, but reading it 100 times had me hurting again.

Me: *You fucked me up so bad. Fuck you Jay, with a long dick.*

I deleted it and turned my phone off then watched Good

Times until I fell back to sleep.

Jay

I stared at the screen, hoping Kola's ass had texted me back, and she didn't. I knew she wouldn't. I don't even know what the hell I was thinking. It was just something about seeing her that made me weak. I had always wanted her back, but now I felt that need for her again that I felt when I first saw her ass. She wasn't happy with that punk ass nigga.

I could tell that Kola seeing Jayson Jr fucked her up. I felt guilty as fuck because I knew it was no way she would get past this shit. I always felt like she would be back, and now, I knew that shit wasn't happening. The bitch Ashley had pulled the ultimate trick, but she had a nigga like me fucked up. I got joint custody and worked out a deal where I bought everything he needed and gave her $400 a month so she wouldn't try to live off a nigga. I tried to explain to the judge how the bitch caught me, but she didn't want to hear my excuses, as she called it.

I loved my son, though. He couldn't do shit but cry, eat, sleep, and shit, but he gave me a sense of pride that I never had. I wished his mother was Kola, but I just had to love him despite the hoe who pushed him out.

"Can you hand me his bag?" I asked Love as she sat on the bed waiting for me to give a fuck about her attitude.

"So, we ain't gonna talk about last night? You basically called me shit in front of your ex. That bitch ain't even all that." She smacked her teeth.

"So, why you mad again?" I asked as I picked up Jayson Jr. and he started chewing on his hand.

197

"So, you still want that bitch?!" she screamed in my face.

I was about to kick her ass out the window in a minute.

"First of all, stop callin' her a bitch because she's far from it, and second, lower your voice in my house before I bust your mouth the fuck open. You hear me?" I asked, looking her dead in the eyes.

"Whatever, Jay. What the fuck you got me around for?" she asked and flopped on the bed.

"Because I like you. I ain't bullshittin' about that."

I kissed her cheek and laid Jayson Jr down. I did like her, but it was far from love. My phone rang next to her, and she rolled her eyes when she looked at the screen. I saw it was that bucket head bitch, Ashley. I was supposed to drop the baby off to her.

"What?" I said.

"Where my son at? You was supposed to have him here an hour ago." She smacked gum or whatever the fuck she was eating in my ear, getting on my fuckin; nerves.

"Y'all bitches testing my patience today," I said before hanging up and looking at Love.

"I gotta go to work. I guess I'ma see you later." She walked by, but I grabbed her arm, pulled her to me, and kissed her.

"I'ma pull up on you, aight?" She nodded and left.

I got lil man together and rolled out. I hated that this bitch lived in the fucking projects with my kid. She had enough money to do better than that. Nickerson Gardens was exactly how it always was. I turned around to look at my son, and I knew I had to get him the fuck out of there. I was gonna tell her that they were gonna move today.

I grabbed my junior and walked up to Ashley's door and

knocked. I could hear movement behind the door, and then the locks turned. When I walked in, clouds of smoke smacked me right in the face.

"Why the fuck would you be smokin' when you knew he was on the way?" I asked, walking in and shaking my head at the poor state of the place.

She had papers all over the couch, and trash all over the floor. Roaches ran up the walls, and I could see them on Jayson Jr's pacifier on the table. I had to tell this bitch too many times to keep this shit clean.

"Man, clean this shit the fuck up," I yelled at her.

"You clean it up, nigga. I worked all damn night." She sat down on the couch.

"What the fuck is all this noise?" Some nigga walked out in a tank top and a pair of khakis.

"Man, what the fuck? Who the fuck is this nigga you got around my son?" I looked at the nigga.

"Man, fuck you and that lil nigga. I'm here for the bitch."

"Mario." Ashley jumped up and pushed him.

He returned with a backhand, and she fell across the couch. I had my son in my arms, and I was ready to drop this nigga. That's why I always kept hands handy. I back up toward the door and whistled loudly. Two niggas who I paid to watch this door at all times since my son lived there came in.

Croc walked up and nodded. He looked like a young Wesley Snipes, with his ugly ass.

Junior already had his pump out. He was older, and was a no bullshit ass nigga.

"Hold my son. Better not drop him either. Take him to my

car," I told Croc, and handed lil Jay to him.

I took the pump from Junior and saw that the chamber was ready to shoot.

"Jay," Ashley pleaded.

"I ain't gonna kill your stupid ass, but this nigga..." I let off a shot right through his heart.

"Nooooo." She cried next to him on the floor.

"Bitch, this ain't no movie. Get your dumb ass up and move around. Police prolly be here soon."

I rolled out and got in the car where my son was securely strapped into his car seat, and drove home. He was never coming back to this bitch either.

*****

Jr was crying his ass off while I got his bottle together. It had been over a month since I had him, and it was hard, but I loved taking care of him. I had even fell back from fucking with the streets for a minute until I got him straight. My lil cousin, Mercy, was about to start watching him for me. She was in college, and she needed the money, so I was gonna pay her and shit. Ashley kept calling me, so I blocked her ass. She needed to do better, and I might let her see him.

"Here you go, lil man."

I held him and fed him his bottle. I couldn't help but think about Kola. I had fucked up any chance of getting her back, but I still couldn't fully let her go. I felt like she rightfully was mine, and she was supposed to be her ass with me. It drove me crazy thinking about not being able to touch her again, and now that she saw I had a kid, I might not ever.

I turned on some cartoons and put lil Jay in his rocker after he drank his bottle. I grabbed my phone and called Duane to see where his fat ass was because that San Fran shipment wasn't there yet, and since I had been staying low, I needed him on point.

"Wassup?" He answered the phone breathing heavily.

"Nigga, I know you ain't fuckin'. You supposed to be on the way here," I barked at him.

"Nah, I just had to whoop Tiffany's ass, man."

"Man, what the fuck?" I hung up on his ass and called Q.

"What's hood, my G?" he answered.

"San Fran all you, bruh. Duane ain't movin' right. Run that shit for me and check on that shipment," I said and hung up with nothing else to discuss.

I didn't give a fuck who you were. If you ain't working, you ain't eating.

****

I had heard that Kola opened up a shop, so I went to corner her ass into talking to me. I knew I should just let her go, but I couldn't. I had Mercy watching lil Jay so I could move around a little bit. This was the first stop I wanted to make. I got out and smiled at the title of the shop. It read *Ms. Kola's Hair Salon.* I guess she was serious about leaving the game, but if I knew her, she wasn't gonna stay gone for long.

I knew she could do more than move weight and pimp, but she was a beast at the shit. When I got to the door, I saw all the bitches, stylists and clients smile and give me them fuck me tonight eyes. I opened the door, and a Spanish chick ran up and put her hands on her hips.

"Hey, your locs don't need re twisting, so I guess you here to see one of us," she boldy stated.

"Nah, I'm here to see Kola." I pushed my hands into my jeans.

"Oh, she in her office." Her smile faded and she walked off.

I walked to the back and saw a door that read owner. I knocked two times.

"Come in," I heard her beautiful voice say.

I turned the knob and smiled. She had a buffalo wing in her hand, with her favorite blue cheese dip dripping off her fingers. The sauce was all over her mouth.

"I see wings still don't stand a chance with you," I said, causing her to hit her knee on the desk trying to get up.

"Why the fuck you here, Jay?" she asked, wiping her mouth and hands with a napkin.

I quickly closed the door and locked it.

"You can't talk to me? It's been long enough." I sat in a chair right in front of the door, blocking her exit.

"No, for what? Like you said, it's been a damn year now. What we need to talk about?" she asked with the pain I caused on her face.

"I know what I did to you."

"No, you don't know what you did. You had me thinking that since you chased me so hard, that meant you would be the best thing that ever happened to me. You left your job for me, you pumped the streets for oil so I could shine with you, and no matter how hard I rode for you, I still wasn't good enough to be the only one. I questioned my looks and who the fuck I was because of you. You did a lot more than cheat." She wiped her eyes and got up.

"I pay for that shit every day I don't have you, Kola. Every fuckin' day I'm reminded of what I fucked up. I had to see you." I got up and walked to her, and she backed up.

"You got a baby now. That seemed to be all you wanted from me, and now you got one. What you want from me now?" She leaned her head to the side, emotionless now.

"You."

I grabbed her shirt and pushed my tongue into her mouth. She let me kiss her for a second, and then pushed me back, slapping me across the face.

"You had me. Now can you leave," she said and sat back down in her chair.

"Love you." I walked out and stood at the door, wondering if I should go back in.

Right before I walked off, I heard, "I love you too," through the door.

I pushed my fist to the door and walked off with a smile at least knowing she still loved me too.

****

"Man, that's fucked up. We blood, nigga." Duane was pissed that I sat him down, but fuck that, I had even more reason to since my shipment disappeared again.

"Fuck that, nigga. You fuckin' up, and if you was one of them other mufuckas, you'd be dead, cuh. That's real talk."

"Man fuck you then, nigga. I can do my own thing," he said and got up.

"And who gon plug you?" I asked.

"That's cool, Jay. Fuck you," he said and walked out my house.

I didn't give a fuck. I knew I felt like that shit wasn't right the first time I went to the bay. I wished I had my bitch here to help me get my head right. She always knew what to do to get my head clear. I could hear Lil jay crying from the den, so I went to get him before he had a fucking fit.

"Damn, nigga. Your ass stink," I said smelling that he shitted.

I grabbed his wipes and diapers. My phone started to ring and I saw it was Colby.

"My nigga." I answered, cradling my phone in my ear while I changed lil man.

"Aye, you need to hit the block tonight, my nigga," he said, sounding hype.

"Nigga, you know I got my lil homie," I said, referring to lil Jay.

"I know. Get Mercy noddle head ass over there. Issa party, my nigga. You been in the house like Betty Crocker and shit, bruh. Come out," he said and hung up.

I chuckled and put my phone down.

I needed to go buy some more diapers and shit for lil man, so I loaded him into the car and went to grab him some shit. I headed to the nearest Walmart and loaded him up. I grabbed some more baby food and milk too. I was walking down the toy aisle when I saw Tiffany in the electronics section. She had on sunglasses, and her lip was busted.

"Tiff," I called out to her.

She looked at me and put on a weak smile.

"Wassup, Jay?" She tried not to look at me.

"You good?"

"No, your brother is a piece of shit, and I'm done with him. He beat me because I saw that he had that bitch, Yvonne, pregnant. He told this bitch they could be his side family. What kind of shit is that, Jay? I'm done with him, though. I took my shit and rolled.

"Damn, well if you need some help, I got you," I told her.

"Thank you. You always been a better man than him. You got fucked up ways, but at least you own it. Don't tell him you saw me, please," she said and backed away.

"And Jay, you need to watch your back. He says some crazy shit sometimes."

She walked off, and it let me know I wasn't feeling the way I had been feeling for no reason. That nigga was up to something.

I hit my nigga Wakeen and told him to follow Daune in so many words. I never spoke direct over the phone. I would find out what his dumb ass was up to, and if I didn't like it, he wouldn't like me.

*****

It was 7 o'clock the next night, and I was supposed to meet up with Missile at 9:00, but I wanted to get ready and shit and give mercy time to get there. I picked lil Jay up and handed him his teething ring.

"Daddy gonna go kick it tonight, if that's cool with you." I tickled his stomach, and he laughed.

He looked just like my ass, and he had my eyes too. He was gonna pull bitches left and right when he got older.

I fed him and texted Mercy. Of course, she jumped at the

chance to make some money. She showed up in like twenty minutes ready.

"I left you some weed too, but smoke that shit when he goes to sleep, and out back," I told her.

"Duh, I got this. You can go get ready." She rolled her eyes and picked lil Jay up.

I jumped in the shower and got dressed, ready to chill. I grabbed my grey Tom Ford tank top and my new Diesel jeans. I had just bought the 8s, and they happened to be grey, so I set them bitches out too.

Before I got in the shower, I texted Kola.

My wife: I don't give a fuck if I seem like a bitch for chasing you, but I'm still on the chase. You my bitch, and I heard you say you loved me too. If you up to holla at me, meet me on Grape tonight.

I put my phone down and went back to getting ready. I hoped she would pop up on a nigga. I know she thinking now.

Duane

Jay had a nigga fucked all the way up. I wasted no time calling my mans Ali, he was one of the Muslim niggas Jay ain't wanna deal with. They paid well, though. All those lost shipments went to them, and I let the foot soldiers take the fall. I let him know I was about to be king of LA, and Jay had to go. Blood or not.

I pulled into my driveway and sat in the car for a minute before going in. I knew Tiffany was probably still pissed for making me beat her ass, but she talked to much, and was too nosey. She was in my phone and saw Yvonne text me, and tried to fake snap on a nigga. I didn't like that shit, so I taught the bitch to leave my phone the fuck alone.

I got out, walked up the stairs, and used my key to enter.

"Tiff," I called out.

She didn't answer; she was probably ignoring me. I jogged up the stairs and went into the bedroom where I saw the closet and drawers open. All of her shit was gone.

"Fuck." I took my phone out and called her. It rang about four times before it picked up.

"Leave my fuckin' daughter alone, you fat bitch. You think she a punching bag?" I heard her mother say.

"Man, that bitch can tell me to leave her alone. Don't make me come fuck you like you wanted when I first met. Should I tell her how you tried to throw pussy at me?" I laughed into the phone.

"Don't call her again." She ignored me and hung up.

Tiffany would be back.

My phone rang, and I saw it was July, a lil bitch from around our old way who I still put the dick in sometimes.

"Yeah?" I answered as I went in the drawer to get a Hershey with almonds.

"Your brother and his friends got some shit going on tonight. My girl, Janay, said all them niggas gon' be out there."

"Oh aight, that's a bet. Thanks boo, what you boutta do?" I asked like I gave a fuck.

"Gonna get my hair done. This new spot got bitches lookin' Hollywood."

"Well, I'm boutta send you some money on that cash app. It's on me." I ate my candy bar and turned the TV on.

"Awww, thank you," she said and I hung up and sent her $500 three times.

Then, I called Yvonne. She was gonna move her position up since Tifanny wanted to be a broke bitch living with her mother.

"Daddy!" she answered excitedly.

"Yeah, you tryna move in with a nigga? I kicked Tiffany out," I lied.

"Oh my God, you got rid of her for me? Hell yeah, let's do it."

"Aight, I'ma send my friends to come help you get your shit."

"Okay, love you."

"See you soon."

I hung up and hit my man, Chop, to go get her shit. I loved

having an in house bitch.

An hour later, my phone rang again. I perked up when I saw that Ali was calling. That meant my payment was ready. He confirmed that I had eight hundred thousand dollars with my name on it. I got up, and took my key off the chain, and slid it under the mat outside for Yvonne.

I pulled up to the mosque and parked in the lot next to an 86 Cadillac on 24s, that bitch was clean. I got out and walked to the side door and hit the buzzer. The door opened, and Ali greeted me with a nod.

"As-salamu alaykum." He waved me in.

"Yeah, so where my money at?" I asked, cutting straight to it.

I was stopped and searched for guns as soon as I got to the back.

"You think I'm coming to start shit when I'm getting paid? Damn, bruh, no honor amongst thieves." I chuckled.

"I don't even trust my mama," he replied.

I followed him to a room with his boss, Shereef, was sitting at a glass desk with a suitcase full of money.

"Duane, smart brother makes smart moves. Almost a million dollars richer. I hope when you take over, you can keep the quality of that shit up." Shareef sat forward with his hands folded on the desk.

"I can guarantee it," I said, going for the money.

"You wanna count it?" Shareef asked.

"Nah, I trust you." I closed the suitcase and stood up.

"What's the situation with your brother?" he asked.

I knew what he meant.

"He out, he gonna be on Grape street tonight, shit you can get a few of them niggas out there and free up some blocks.

"Cold blooded. I don't trust you, Duane. You would kill your own brother, so why wouldn't you kill me? I trust the product, though. we can take care of your brother." One of his men came and stood next to me. I guess that was my cue to go.

"Aight."

I left with my money, and didn't give two fucks about his lil speech. I went straight home and saw that Yvonne's car was there. I rang the bell since I left her the key. She opened the door all smiles and had the house smelling like she was cooking.

"Hey daddy, welcome home." She smiled. I saw her small stomach and touched my growing child.

"I can get used to this shit." I kissed her and walked in to get to my safe.

"So, what you got in there?" She came behind me.

"None of your business. Go sit down until I come get you.

She went back down the stairs, and I went to my room in the closet and turned the false wall. I had two safes in there. I put the whole suitcase in the safe and backed before moving the clothes back. When I got down stairs, I heard Yvonne in the kitchen on the phone.

"Yeah, I just moved in. I'm happy as hell," she said, smiling from ear to ear.

When I got to her, I smiled then slapped the shit out of her.

She looked genuinely confused.

"Didn't I tell you to sit down and wait for me to get you?" I asked, stroking her face.

"But I was cooking, and—" I cupped her face and kissed her.

"I'm sorry, just don't start thinkin' when I say shit that I don't mean it. I gotta run, I'ma be back." I kissed her and left out again.

I wanted to be there to make sure Jay's ass died. I couldn't have any mistakes. I was meant to be the king of California.

Kola

I tapped my finger on the desk as I read the text Jay sent. Then, I went to my messages and listened as Derrick begged me to call him. I wasn't talking to his stupid ass right now. Again, my love life was trash. Derrick got drunk and crashed his truck into my damn car. I had given up on him, and now I just wanted him to leave me the hell alone. I locked my phone when my office door opened and in walked Kammi. She looked irritated.

"What's wrong?" I asked her.

"This bitch out here got on my last nerve while she was waiting. All her ugly ass wants is a sew-in. Please, take her," Kammi begged.

"Aight."

I hated loud bitches like the one she talking about. They sit on the phone and let the world know the conversation and shit.

"We closing in two hours. They wait to walk in and shit."

I got up and went out to the front. The salon was empty, and the only person sitting in the chair was the loud heffa who was still talking on the phone. I was glad she had been shampooed and dried.

"Yes, bitch, he sent 1500 dollaaaaassssss. You know we getting' fucked up tonight, girl." The girl sounded like a loud speaker.

Kammi grabbed her purse and waved bye. I locked the door behind her.

"Um, 'scuse me, but can we get this shit poppin'? I got moves," she said to me.

"Girl, bye." I rolled my eyes.

She smacked her teeth and returned to her conversation. I started the braid in her hair and she started doing the most running her nigga's business.

"Girl, his ass boutta wife me, bitch."

I continued the braids, and was ready to choke this bitch.

"Whole time, though, he boutta run these streets, baby. His brother don't even know what's comin'. I'ma act surprised as shit tonight," she said.

I shook my head because this bitch could be getting recorded, and she spilling everything.

"Where the hair?" I interrupted her.

She handed it to me from off the floor, and I took it out and laid the packs of hair on my table. It was green and orange. Ratchet hoes.

"Yeah, the light skin one with dreads. You should have fucked his ass when I told you to get at him. He had a bitch, but I think he single now. It ain't gon' matter after tonight. Damn, Jay is fine, though."

She stopped to let the other person talk, and I thought she could be talking about Jayson, but I didn't know. I was damn sure about to find out.

"Aye, you know this dude name Duane?" I asked, like it wasn't life and death for her.

"Hold on, girl," she told her friend.

"Yeah, that's my dude." She looked me up and down.

"And his brother is Jay, right?" I asked like I was still innocent.

"Yeah, damn. You FBI? Shit." She put the phone back to her ear.

"Damn, I need to get thread," I said and walked to the back to get my gun. I grabbed my .40 and walked back out.

"Bitch, get up," I said, wasting no time pressing the piece to the back of her dome.

I snatched the phone out her hand and stomped it.

"Walk to the back," I ordered.

She had tears falling from her eyes, and the weave was dragging from her head behind her.

"I don't know why you doin' this." She sniffled.

"I'm Kola, Jay's ex. Now what the fuck is Duane planning tonight?" I asked once I got her out back by the trash cans.

"I don't know, but he said that he would be on Grape tonight with Jay, and some shit supposed to go down." She backed up as I attached the silencer.

"Aight. That's a bet."

I shot her in the head and watched her body drop. I quickly called my clean up crew and told them they had to be there asap. Beverly Hills wasn't the type of place that won't call the police when they see a body. I called Jay after turning the lights out and grabbing the bitch's purse and phone.

Jay's phone went straight to voicemail. His shit must have died. I got in my car and drove to Jay's house to see if he was there before I went to Grape. I pulled into the driveway and saw a car I didn't recognize. After ringing the bell, I waited, and a girl answered holding Jayson's son.

"Hi, I'm—"

"Kola. It's me, Mercy. I lost some weight, but we met at my uncle's surprise party like two years ago." She smiled.

"Oh yeah. Hey, is Jay here?" I asked, looking around the home we once shared.

I looked at the couch where we made love endless times. Shit, even the tables.

"No, he left. His charger is here, so I think his phone died."

"You got Duane's number by any chance?" I pulled my phone out. I had his old number, I already tried it.

"Yeah." She went in her phone and read it off to me.

"Thanks," I said and walked away.

"He talks about you a lot. I can tell he still loves you," she said, stopping me.

"I couldn't tell." I got in the car and called Duane's grimy ass.

"Hello," he answered, sounding like he was eating.

"Duane, where the fuck is Jay?" I based on him.

"Bitch, don't be callin' my phone begging for no dick." He laughed.

I could hear Jay in the background talking.

"Who dat, nigga?" Jay asked.

"This bitch that won't get off my dick." Duane hung up.

I was gonna kill that motherfucker. I didn't even know if Jayson deserved the loyalty I was showing his stupid ass.

I needed to get some niggas to roll with me, but I know I didn't have any guns for them. I hated that I had to call the only person who could get me together real quick, especially since I had been giving him the cold shoulder.

The phone rang twice, and Derrick picked up.

"I been hoping I would hear from you, bae. I wanna say sorry. Can I come through?"

"Yeah, whatever. I need to talk to you."

"Where you at? I'm at Lee's," he said.

"Stay there." I hung up.

I didn't need his sorry. I just wanted to grab some steel and fix this bullshit.

I smoked one of my pre-rolled blunts on the way to calm my nerves. I was so scared I wouldn't make it. I tried to call Jay again, but it went to voicemail again.

I saw Derrick's F150 parked in two spaces like he always did when he drove it. I got out and went to the passenger side and knocked on the window. When the door unlocked, I hopped in and was greeted with the smell of fried chicken.

"Damn, you look good," he said and reached for me.

"I just need some help. I need a few guns, and I got you when I get to my safe," I said, cutting his game.

"Damn, straight business, huh. Come on, why we gotta be fucked up? I ain't drank shit since you backed off me. Ion wanna keep losin' you."

"I'm sorry, but I ain't fuckin' with me and you, Derrick. Ain't like you a terrible dude, but we can't be shit as long as you drinkin'. Now, can you help me, please?" I asked and folded my arms.

"Yeah, man, I got some shit in the trunk," he said with a nasty attitude before he got out and took the cover off the bed of his pick up. He dropped the small door and slid a green trunk out to the edge.

"Pop the trunk," he demanded, and I did it.

Derrick put the trunk in the back, and without another word, got into his truck. Smoke filled the air as he burned rubber, zoomed out the space, and drove off. I didn't come to piss him off, but he had to know it wasn't an us anymore and never would be.

I shot a text to Marco and Denzel, two niggas I never fully let go of on my team. They still did what they did best, but I didn't use them a lot since Jay liked using his own niggas. They had guns, but I liked to give them mine so I can take them and destroy the shit myself after shit is taken care of. They, of course, hit me back with a quickness. I let them know what corner I wanted to meet at, and I also had another favor.

****

Marco stood his big, ugly, sexy ass across from me with his best friend, Denzel, next to him. I know it sounds crazy calling him sexy and ugly, but that he was. His face wasn't sexy, but his body and demeanor was. He carried himself like a true thug, and it was sexy on him.

"Ms. Kola, I was all smiles when you called." He showed his perfect white teeth.

"Well, I'm all for that smile," I flirted.

"So, what you need from us, baby girl," Denzel said, breaking up the banter.

"Jay in some shit. I need y'all to come through for me and stop some shit his brother set up tonight. And that special thing. I need all them niggas wiped out. I hear one of the lead niggas is a dude named Ali. I want them all," I said and grit my teeth.

"What you got for us?" Marco asked, walking past me and opening the trunk that contained whatever Derrick had in there.

"Damn." Denzel reached in and pulled out an large automatic bad motherfucker. There were two more of those two pumps, and a few hand guns.

"Shit, we set." Marco nodded.

"Okay, let's go. Y'all can decide where y'all wanna stand," I said, looking at my phone as Goose called me.

"Cuz, you picked a fucked up time," I said as I started the car back.

"Kola, where you at?" he asked, sounding like shit was gonna get more fucked up.

"I got some shit to handle. Why, wassup?" I asked.

"You on a hit list, Kola. You and that nigga Jay, it just came across me. Where you at?"

Boom

I dropped and turned around, only to see Denzel approaching me with his gun drawn.

"I'm sorry, Kola, I swear. If it was any different, we could have been some real shit, but you worth a million, boo." Marco lifted his gun to shoot me, but he was sent flying back.

Two more guns shots, and Marco went down before he knew what hit him.

"Kola, come on," I heard Sammi say.

"How—"

"You think he ain't been making sure you good?" he asked and pushed me into my car then jumped in the passenger side. I

I saw my phone on the ground, so I got out snatched it and my guns from Marco and Denzel's dead bodies. I couldn't believe them niggas. I ain't been shit but good to them.

"Man, what the fuck was that shit, Kola? If I wasn't here, you woulda been laid the fuck out." Sammi said and pulled his phone out.

"We need to get to Jayson like now," I said with tears falling down my face.

"Calm down. I'm sorry, Kola," Sammi said and put the gun to the side of my head.

"Sammi, what the fuck?" I said and looked at him in complete shock.

"I have too."

He cracked me over the head, and I blacked out.

Jay

It was good getting out the house and chilling with my niggas. I felt what females say when they want to get out after having a kid all day. I had to go in my homie Kane spot to see if my phone was fully charged so I could check on lil man. Duane walked right behind me This nigga was on some other shit, and I could feel it. After what Tiffany said, and all the other shit I've been thinkin', I knew something wasn't right.

"You know you boutta be an uncle," he said, telling me something I already knew.

I still acted surprised and shit.

"That's wassup, cuh," I said and turned my phone on.

"So, who got lil Jay?" he asked.

I turned to him, wondering why the fuck he gave a shit where my son was.

"Mercy, why?" I asked, sounding defensive and not giving a fuck.

"Damn, I'm just talkin'. We was just talkin' about babies, nigga," he said and walked out the room.

I felt this gut instinct telling me I needed to get home. As soon as I walked out the room, I saw a voicemail pop up from Kola. I put the phone to my ear.

"Jay, Duane is setting you up—"

I couldn't hear the rest of the message because the gun cocking behind me took precedence.

"That bitch called you too, huh?" I heard Duane say from behind me.

"I ain't wanna believe the shit." I chuckled and turned around.

"You should have fuckin' known. You tried to treat me like a fuck boy, but I couldn't let you. You wouldn't take the bait with those texts about your father, so—"

"That was you, nigga?"

"Yeah." He laughed. "That nigga died last year, ain't leave you shit and still didn't give a shit."

"You was always jealous of me, nigga. You ain't boutta make it out here alive, even if I don't. All my niggas out there." I nodded, trying to think of a quick way to get his fat ass.

I started to hear gun fire outside. Duane stood there, smiling like it was all part of his plan.

He continued to talk.

"Like your man, Sammi? Ali got a price on you and that bitch head, and I just got a text that they got Kola's sexy ass. They might take turns beating that pussy up before they kill her. With y'all gone, we open for business."

My head started to feel dizzy when he said they had Kola.

"Quiet now, Jay? Well, this should get you talkin'. I already got Yvonne going to pick lil Jay up. I can raise him in your absence. Don't worry, though, I'ma let him know his father was a G."

I didn't blink before I charged him, but I wasn't quick enough. He was able to get my thigh, but I got to him.

"Shoot him!" Duane yelled to somebody.

I jumped up to see the niggas in thobes and kufis.

"I'ma see you in hell, lil bro," I spit at him right before I heard the shot.

I braced myself, but the gunshots continued, and I still wasn't hit.

"Y'all had me fucked up!" I heard Kola yell following the gun shots.

Duane tried to run to the back, but I kicked him in the ankle. I heard the snap as my foot connected.

"Baby." I ran up to Kola and was more than surprised when she pushed her tongue into my mouth.

"I love you, bae," I told her.

"I love you too, mufucka."

She slapped the shit out of me and pushed me. I was confused as she ran out the door. I almost forgot Duane was on the ground behind me.

"Fuck you, Jay." He spit on me as I approached.

"You already fucked me. So, you was behind it all, huh?" I started stomping his ankle.

"See, I ain't like you. Ain't gonna kill you, I just want you watching your back for the rest of your life. I want it to be a surprise, lil bro." I left the room and saw bodies everywhere, but I went looking for Kola.

Police were heading my way, and I looked around to find Kola before they showed up. As I tried to run, I saw Q laying on the ground, eyes wide open, with blood draining from his mouth.

"Fuck!" I yelled, but I had to keep going.

"Jay," I heard somebody say.

I turned around and saw Ashley standing there with a gun pointed right at me.

"This some funny shit." I chuckled.

"I want my son." She breathed heavily, and I noticed her eyes were red and bugged out.

"My son staying with me. Go the fuck home," I said, getting closer to her.

"He ain't your son, dummy." She started laughing.

"Bitch, we did a DNA test. Fuck you mean?" I was in pain because of the gun shot, but I was about to whoop her ass.

"The paper you got in the mail was fake, nigga, I just needed a come up."

I started toward her, and the bitch shot me in the chest. She ran off just as I fell. I couldn't move after I hit the pavement.

Kola

I went to get my car so I could come back and get Jay. He was bleeding, so I knew he was hurt. I loved that nigga, and stupid or not, we were going to be good. I drove down the street I ran down and saw a bitch running with a gun. When I saw what she was running from, I threw the car into park and jumped out.

"Baby no, you can't do this to me." I pulled his head up and watched him try to talk.

"I swear... I swear, I loved you, girl." He closed his eyes tight because of the pain he was in.

"I love you too, but I told you, I won't let you die." I tried with all my might to lift him, but I couldn't.

I looked to the sky.

"You can't do this again. You can't do this shit to me again," I cried to God.

"Shit, Jay."

I saw Jay's friend, Missile, running toward me.

"Help him. Put him in the car," I screamed.

Once he got him in the car, I pulled my gun out the glove box.

"Man, what the fuck, Kola?" He held his hands up.

"I had to kill Sammi for trying to kill me, and I will kill you dead if you think you hurting me or him," I said with a tear sliding down my face.

"It's me, Kola. You gonna let him die?" he asked, looking sincere, but fuck that.

"Just go!" he yelled.

I put the gun down and peeled out. I drove straight toward Killer King. I didn't want to take him there, but I had no choice.

"You good, baby. I promise, I got you," I told Jay as he lay in the passenger side bleeding out.

"Fuck, baby." He coughed up blood and winced in pain.

"It's okay, Jay," I cried as I whipped through the streets trying to get to the hospital.

"I love you. This is why I wanted you to have my baby, Kola," he said with tears.

"I couldn't, because of this, Jay. I was pregnant before, and when Anthony died, so did the baby. I can't go through this again, so you see, you gotta live. I will give you 100 kids, just please, don't die." I swung the car into the ER entrance.

"Here, I need you to go get my son," he said, trying to go into his pocket. He slowly pulled out a box and handed it to me.

"It's because I want to," he said and slowly closed his eyes.

"Jay, no!" I jumped out and called out to the fuckin' staff on a smoke break out front.

The got him on a gurney and whisked him in. I tried to run back there with him, but they stopped me.

"Get the fuck out my way!" I screamed to the bitch who was about to get knocked the fuck out.

"We can't let you back there," she yelled in my face. I reared my hand back, but my hand was caught by security.

The bitch smirked.

I made a photo memory of her face and went to the waiting room. When I opened the box and saw the ring, I dissolved into tears as I shook my head. Then, I remembered what Jay said about getting his son. I didn't want to leave him, but I had to. I left and got in the car heading toward the house. I swear, I don't know how I got there, but I did.

"What the fuck?" I said aloud after seeing the same girl who shot Jay.

I blocked the car she was getting into and jumped out. I could hear the baby crying in the back seat, then I put it together. This was the bitch. I wasn't impressed by far, but it didn't matter at this point. When she saw me coming, she pulled out the same gun I saw her running with.

"You shot my nigga?" I asked, smiling and nodding my head.

"Your nigga?" She laughed maniacally.

"Yeah, mine, bitch." I was quick draw like a cowboy movie, and shot her in the hand she held the gun in.

"I'm glad he's dead," she said, laughing and crying from the pain. "He only wanted some fat bitch when he had all this shit."

"I ain't fat, bitch, I'm thick." I shot her right in the nose, and it went out the back of her head.

"Waaaaah, waaahhhhhhh." I heard the baby crying from the car.

I quickly unstrapped him and grabbed the car seat. I stopped in my tracks to the car when I saw feet hanging out the door.

"Mercy," I said and ran to the door, only to see a pregnant woman laid on her back dead.

Who the fuck is this?

I thought to myself as I pushed the door open further to see

Mercy with a hole in the side of her head. I closed my eyes and left because one of them had released their bowels, and it was making me sick. I called the police for them to deal with this shit.

"Come on, lil man. We gonna go see your daddy," I said.

Jay had a whole baby on my ass, and here I was trying to do him right. I didn't know what to do but sit in my car and think before pulling off. I didn't think I would ever take him back, ever and I still didn't know. I took my phone out my glove box and called Jay's mom.

"Hi, Kola," she said like I irritated her.

"Jay is in King. That bitch shot him."

"I bet you had something to do with the shit. Soon as—"

"Shut that shit up. I never got what your fuckin' problem was, but you got me fucked up!" I yelled at her.

"Oh, shut the fuck up. I only fuck with you cuz I like ya. I told Jay he was a damn fool. Well, I'm gonna call Duane to pick me up," she said.

"Duane was the one who set him up." I said and hung up when I saw a call from Shay.

"Shay, Jay got shot." I felt emotional all over again.

"Bitch, what? Where y'all at?" she asked.

"King, come on." I cried again.

"I gotta pick up Diamond," she said, sounding like she was smoking

"Just come the fuck on." I hung up and took a deep breath.

I drove back to the hospital and parked then grabbed the baby from the back seat. I didn't even know his name.

I walked in and saw the bitch who stopped me from going back the first time. I was gonna beat her ass once I found out Jay was good.

"Aye." Missile said.

I felt so bad for how I treated him earlier.

"I'm so—"

"It's cool. I heard you put some hot ones in Sammi, just like you said. Never trusted him," he said and looked at the baby.

"I knew Jay a long time. I mean, I've seen him in love, I've seen him just wanting to fuck bitches, but he was hooked on your without words or contact before he even pursued your ass. I know my word don't mean shit to you, but he ain't love that bitch. He fucked up like we all do. If he walks out, this his second chance." He sat back in the chair and waited. A few more of his people showed up, and then his mother.

"Kola. Why you got little Jay? Where Mercy?" she asked, running up and taking the little boy.

It's not like I forgot about Mercy but I was just focused on Jay.

"The girl killed her and some pregnant broad at the house."

"What? Why the hell didn't you tell me?" she screamed, causing the baby to cry.

I took him because he was reaching for me and clearly afraid.

"Mam, you came in with Jayson Wells?" An old Indian man with blue scrubs and a white mask pulled under his chin came up to me.

"Yes. What happened?" I asked, already expecting the worse.

"He pulled through, but he needs blood. We need to test to see if anybody's a match.

"I don't like needles," Ms Anne said, straightening up from her crying spell.

"Why wouldn't you want to so we can save his life? Come on, we all doin' it," I demanded.

I was happy to see a few more of Jay's family come in. Diamond and Shay showed up right before I went to hvave blood drawn. I looked at Diamond, who had a large black eye that she was trying to cover with makeup.

"Hey, bitches." I smiled, trying to hold back tears. I was happy he was still alive, but I was still scared for him.

Hours later, they still wouldn't let us back, and I was getting irate as a motherfucker. We did the blood and everything, and still nothing. I started to stomp toward the nurse's window when I saw the doctor coming back out. The police came in, and I thought I was about to get locked the fuck up for that OK Corral shit I did.

"Carla Palton." They came up to Jayson's mother and grabbed her up.

"No, no! He's mine, that bitch tried to take my husband." She jumped up and down.

Who the fuck is Carla?

I thought to myself. I always knew her as Francis.

"What the hell is goin' on?" I ask the two of them.

"Carla Palton murdered her husband's mistress and cut the baby right out of her. She hadn't been seen in almost 30 years until the DNA hit a match in." He put cuffs on her.

"Wait, so you was the wife, and you stole Jay?" I asked, looking at her in disbelief. This shit was gonna devastate him.

"This shit all yur fuckin' fault. You should have stayed the fuck away from my son." She kicked at me and the clocked her on the head and dragged her out the door.

"What the fuck just happened." I said looking at the people who claimed to be Jays family.

"We didn't know, we swear. She came here with him when he was a baby and she said she left her husband." Jays cousin Jewels spoke up.

"This shit too much." I put my free hand on my head like it would stop my head from throbbing.

"You were a match for his blood type." The doctor came up to me.

"Okay, let's do it," I said now not even thinking about am shit that just went down.

"Missile, hold him and don't let none of these fraud mufuckas touch him," I said to him. I didn't give a fuck that they heard me either. I still didn't trust them regardless of them claiming not to know.

I went to a room where they drained me of so much blood I felt dizzy and sick when they were done. I prayed to God, my father, and even Anthony to look out for him.

Jay

My chest felt like it was on fire when I opened my eyes and realized that bitch didn't kill me.

"There go daddy."

I heard Kolas voice and looked over to see her holding lil Jay.

"Bae, you ain't let me die." I smiled, attempting humor.

"I don't care how much I hate your ass for what you did, I wouldn't let that happen. Now you really got my blood running through your veins," she said with her lips pressed together like she was about to cry.

"I'm sor—"

She got up and put her finger over my mouth.

She gave me my water and put the straw to my mouth. My mouth was dry as shit, so it was the best shit I ever tasted in my life.

"I got some shit to tell you," she said, sitting down and taking a deep breath.

"The bitch that shot you killed Mercy and some pregnant broad at your house."

"What! Man, fuck, I swear I can't wait to get up so I can get that bitch." I said, feeling like a raging bull.

"I got her ass already, cuh. If any bitch gonna kill you, it's gon be me if you ever do me dirty again, nigga, you hear me?" she said, looking me dead in my eyes.

"It's something else," she said and hesitated.

"Say it, what the fuck!" I said, raising my voice.

"Your mother is not your mother, she was your father's wife and she killed your mother and stole you. Her real name is—"

"Carla," I said and closed my eyes, trying to understand what the fuck I was just told. I couldn't even put the shit together in my mind. That meant Duane ass wasn't my blood brother, and I should have killed his ass when I had the chance. It took me a few hours to compose myself before I told Kola what I had to tell her.

After my people left, I let lil Jay sit on the bed with me while Kola went to get us something for her and lil Jay to snack on. I couldn't believe he wasn't mine, and it was crazy that he actually looked like me. That bitch got my ass good but she at least helped me realize that shit ain't always about me. I love him even though he ain't my blood. I was still gonna do another test to make sure, but I was keeping him regardless, and I hoped that if Kola was coming home she would accept him. It's asking a lot, but she seems to be in love with him too from how she interacts with him.

Missile told me I was out for two days, and she kept him with her. I felt like shit knowing she still had the hurt then had to assume responsibility for my fuck up.

"I got you a water even though you could get it free from the nurses." She walked in and swooped lil Jay up and opened him and apple juice.

"She said he wasn't mine," I said, not really sure how to start the conversation.

Kola looked at me through squinted eyes. "And that was the type of hoe you wanted." I could tell that pissed her off.

"No, I didn't. I want you, I always did. I read that letter you left on your old dude's grave a few years ago.

She looked like she was trying to remember, and then gave me another angry glare.

"You had no right to do that shit, nigga!" She raised her voice.

"Calm the fuck down and come sit down," I said, not playing with her ass at all.

She did what I said and sat next to me.

"I saw how much love you could have, and it made me want that shit from you. I needed that shit. We can raise him, we can get married and do whatever the fuck you want, just take me back. I can't live right without my bitch by my side. Look how you ran into a house full of niggas. You ain't ready to stop us."

"Jay—"

"Nah, I let you have all that space, and even didn't kill the nigga for snatchin' you up, baby girl. This shit ends now. You gonna bring your ass home, fuck everybody but us. You hear me, Kola, fuckem. Don't ever lie to me again, and I won't ever hurt you again." I gathered all my strength and pulled her to me then pushed my tongue in her mouth.

She bit my lip

"I hate you, but I love you more." She came back and kissed me again.

This was our new beginning, and this time, shit was gon' be right. I was gonna get lil Jay tested again by somebody I trusted this time just to make sure.

***

6 months later

Before I left the hospital, I had a nigga from forensics who I was cool with to come swab me and lil Jay. I got the results back in a few hours, and lil Jay wasn't mine like that bitch said. It didn't matter, I loved him, and he was staying with me as my son, because that what he was to me.

Kola moved back in, and honestly, I can't say it was easy the first few weeks, but she is starting to forgive me, and that's all I can ask. She said she wasn't ready to be married, and I respected that too.

I went to see Carla in jail, and she apologized for what she did. She was the only mother I knew, and she gave me a good life, so I couldn't complain about shit she ever did, but she still robbed me of knowing my real parents and I couldn't say that shit was cool.

I found out that Duane didn't know what the fuck he was talking about when it came to my real father. I found out he was an investment banker on Wall Street. I found him and told him who I was, and this nigga was so happy he broke down on the ground crying. He had my eyes, and that shit had me a little emotional.

Kola was supportive as fuck to a nigga too. She helped me find my mother's family and everything. I had to do her right. She deserves every bit of happiness I can give her mean ass.

Duane had the balls to call me begging for forgiveness like a punk ass bitch. I traced the call with this app I got and went to where it led me. As soon as he opened the door, I emptied a whole clip into his ass. I was even more surprised that he didn't bury Yvonne, but instead, he had Tiffany back and living there like the shit didn't matter.

Right now, me and my baby were about to go handle the rest of these mufuckas. Shareef led this shit off, and I was about to get rid of everybody with a kufi that I saw standing outside his spot. I got some good info that he played chess outside every day at 1 o'clock.

"You ready, baby girl?" I asked Kola as she added a new clip on the AR. She looked sexy as a motherfucker too. I had to adjust my dick.

"Yeah, nasty." She cut her eyes and smirked.

"Here we go," I said, slowly creeping around the corner.

I could have sent niggas to do it, but I wanted this for myself, and so did my bitch, so we out there.

As soon as I saw Shareef, I tapped Kola.

"Bitch ass niggas," Kola called out, causing them to look, but they would never get to react. We started spraying they ass. Shareef tried to cut out, but Kola chopped his ass down.

"You the baddest bitch in the world," I told her coolly as we sped off to dump the shit and pick lil Jay up.

I felt better knowing these niggas had paid for what they did. Now I could cool the fuck out.

*****

"So, what you think about goin' with me?" Kola was getting dressed to go visit her ex's grave.

I didn't understand why the fuck she was pressing me to go.

"Man, damn, aight Kola." I jumped up and grabbed Lil Jay off the bed.

"Listen." She looked at me with attitude.

"Shut your ass up and come on, funky ass attitude and shit. You ain't gonna get none actin' like that." I smacked her ass.

"Nigga, I'll hold you at gun point for the dick," she said and kissed me.

"Oh, you did the for that dick challenge, huh?" I laughed.

"Yeah, I ride for that dick, drive for that dick, jump off a roof and fly for that dick, trap for that dick, rap for that dick, do a drive by and shake the ops for that dick," she said and burst out laughing.

"You stupid as shit." I laughed with her. I stopped and saw a genuine smile on her face.

"You ready?" she asked, picking up her purse and holding a letter in her hand.

I nodded and we were out the door.

Kola

As Jay and I approached Anthony's head stone, I got emotional as I always did when I visited. Jay grabbed my hand.

I laid the letter down on the stone and stepped back.

"This is Jay, Ant. He loves me, and I love him so much. He reminds me of you. I can't keep the hold you have on me from starting over, but I will never stop loving you. I just have to let you go, because..."

I grabbed Jay's hand.

"I wanna get married and have a baby without being scared of history repeating itself."

Jay squeezed my hand and smiled.

"I just wanted you to know I was in it. We can start planning and doin' whatever the fuck we need to do, nigga." I lay on his chest as he held lil Jay, and we walked to the car.

"Wait, what was in that letter?" Jay asked as we got inside the car.

"None ya." I smiled as we pulled off to the next grave site. I went to the freshly dug grave with a heavy heart.

"Why couldn't you leave him, Diamond? Look what he did to you." I fell down and cried over my friend's grave.

Raj had stabbed her 67 times for smiling at the gas station attendant. He didn't need to be buried, he was chopped up into pieces and burning in acid as you read this shit. I couldn't let him go sit in a jail cell while she rotted in the ground. That shit just wouldn't work for me.

"Girl, Shay was just talking about you. You know how she do, right?" I said, wishing she would answer me. "She doin' good though, sis. She got big though, she all knocked up." I chuckled.

Jay sat in the car and waited for me as I said my goodbyes to her. We were leaving LA and moving to Dallas, Texas to start over. Jay decided to cut out the game and just invest. He kicked some real ass too when he started letting his father do his investing, We didn't have to work ever again, but I still wanted to have a salon, so I was moving my stylists to Dallas and see where our talent takes us.

As I drove through LA for probably the last time, I got emotional as my life flashed before my eyes. I looked at the nail shop I went into when Derrick came back into my life. I shook my head at the thought of him. I heard he got drunk and drove his car into a police cruiser. They locked his ass up. I was good now. I found some crazy ass type of love, but it works for us. I couldn't wait until we got on the road to Dallas to let Jay know I was pregnant.

The End